DISCOVER GALWAY

PAUL WALSH is an archaeologist with a passionate interest in the local history of his native city, Galway. Since 1981 he has worked with Ordnance Survey Ireland, Dublin, and in 1999 moved to Dúchas, Department of Arts, Heritage, Gaeltacht and the Islands. A member of the board of directors of the Discovery Programme (1996–2001), he is co-director, with Dr E Fitzpatrick, NUI Galway, of the Galway Excavations Project, which, with the assistance of funding from The Heritage Council, is undertaking the publication of archaeological investigations undertaken in the city between 1987 and 1998. His academic interests include Irish prehistory (especially megalithic monuments), medieval architecture, and the archaeology and history of Galway city. He has published widely on all these topics in various books and journals. His other interests include music, especially choral music, and he is musical director of the People's College Choir, Dublin.

Discover GALWAY

PAUL WALSH

THE O'BRIEN PRESS
DUBLIN

First published 2001 by The O'Brien Press Ltd.,
20 Victoria Road, Dublin 6, Ireland.
Tel: +353 1 4923333; Fax: +353 1 4922777
E-mail: books@obrien.ie
Website: www.obrien.ie

ISBN: 0-86278-631-2

British Library Cataloguing-in-Publication Data
A catalogue record for this title is available from the British Library

1 2 3 4 5 6 7 8 9 10
01 02 03 04 05 06 07

The O'Brien Press   the arts
receives assistance fron   council
                                  an chomhairle
                                  ealaíon
                                  50ᵗ

Editing, typesetting, layout and design: The O'Brien Press Ltd.
Modern map of Galway: Design Image
Front cover: bottom photo courtesy Galway Arts Festival;
top image courtesy Derek Biddulph
Cover separations: C&A Print Services Ltd.
Printing: GraphyCEMS

For Anne and Maria,

and in memory of my father and mother

PICTURE CREDITS

The author and publisher wish to thank the following for permission to reproduce visual mate-rial: Derek Biddulph, front cover (top); Galway Arts Festival, front cover (bottom); Paul Duffy, p.54, p.57; Dominic Delany, p.11; Donal Mac Giolla Easpaig, p.8; Galway County Library. p.39; Galway Diocesan Office, p.60, p.116; James Hardiman Library Archives, NUI Galway, p.43; Reproduced courtesy of the Committee of the Galway Archaeological and Historical Society, p.16, p.39 (top); *Connacht Tribune,* p.115; Kenny's Book Shop and Art Gallery, p.63 (bottom); Dúchas, The Heritage Service, p.29, p,81; Ordnance Survey, Ireland, p.67; Bord Fáilte, p.56, p.63 (top), p.75, p.89; Ireland West Tourism, p.62; Courtesy of the National Library of Ireland, p.49 (bottom), p.52 (bottom), p.53, p.54, p.59, p.84, p.95, p.102, p.119; The Board of Trinity College, Dublin, p.20, p.34, p.122; Department of Folklore, UCD, p.97; the British Library, London, p.27; Public Record Office, London, p.25.

All other photos/illustrations copyright of the author.

ACKNOWLEDGEMENTS

The author would like to extend special thanks to the following: Kieran Hoare, Archivist, Hardi-man Library, NUI Galway; Maureen Moran, Galway County Library; Jackie Uí Chionna, Galway Civic Trust; Anne Melia, Ireland West Tourism; Tom May, Diocesan Office, Galway Cathedral; Tom Kenny; Angela Gallagher; Tony Roche and John Scarry, Dúchas; Ronan Fleming, Bord Fáilte; John Browne, National Photographic Archive; Keith Barratt, Design Image; Tom O'Sulli-van for technical assistance with illustrations; Dominic Delany for details of his excavations at Bollingbrook Fort; Peadar O'Dowd and Fr John O'Connor, OSA, for information on Forthill cemetery. An extra-special thanks to my wife, Anne, for her patience and encouragement throughout. This work could not have been brought to fruition without the singular support of the staff at The O'Brien Press, especially Ivan O'Brien (illustrations) and Rachel Pierce whose resourceful editorial guidance and cheerfulness rendered the production process a smooth operation.

CONTENTS

PART ONE: THE HISTORY OF THE CITY

PART TWO: GUIDE TO THE HISTORIC CITY

THE HISTORY OF THE CITY

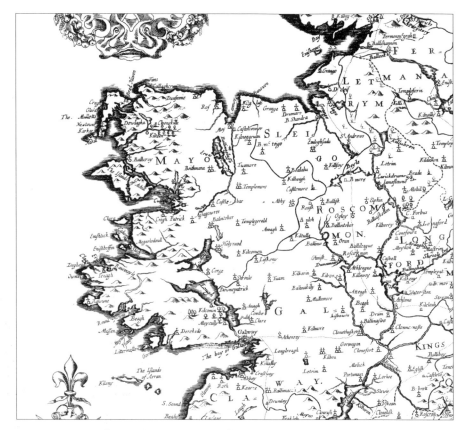

Connacht as represented on William Petty's map of Ireland (1685).

Discover Galway

The writer of a guide book on Galway is faced with a dilemma: how can one capture the blend of past and present that permeates this beautiful city and do equal justice to both? For Galway defies classification. It is full of delights for the stranger and yet there are many surprises for those who consider they know it well. As the capital of Connacht and tourist gateway to Connemara, the Burren and the Aran Islands it has earned a reputation as the most lively and delightful of Irish cities. From humble beginnings it has grown and evolved into a large and prosperous metropolis – the third largest urban centre in Ireland – with a regional airport, extensive harbour facilities, numerous industries, dynamic retail, commercial and services sectors, a university and institute of technology, a cathedral, a well-known seaside suburb (Salthill), a vibrant centre for the arts, a rich architectural heritage and, above all, a fascinating history.

Situated at the inner end of Galway Bay, the city stands at the mouth of the short River Corrib, which flows from the lake of that name into the sea. Both lake and river effectively divide Galway county in two, marking the boundary between the rich, fertile inland country to the east and the mountainous area of Connemara to the west. The bay is sheltered from the fiercest of the Atlantic storms by the three islands of Aran, which form an effective barrier across its mouth. Over the centuries the people of Galway capitalised on its natural setting and the town grew as an effective trading station, developing contacts with the markets of Europe's Atlantic seaboard.

Today's visitor will find Galway much as it must have been in its heyday: a busy working city. The central layout, established in its early years, persists almost unchanged to the present day. Narrow streets, tall buildings, converted warehouses, old archways and charming pubs – all contribute to the mosaic of Galway's teeming history.

Early beginnings

There is a tradition that prior to the establishment of the Anglo-Norman settlement at Galway in the thirteenth century there was formerly a small fishing village here. This early settlement was allegedly known by the name Baile an Sruthán, or the town of the streams, presumably so-called because in winter the river was accustomed to overflow its banks. Whatever the truth of this tradition, Galway first appears in recorded history as the place where, in 1124, the castle of *Bun Gaillimhe* or the mouth of the Galway [river] (now the River Corrib) was erected for Turlough O'Connor, king of Connacht. At that time the area around the present-day city formed part of the territories controlled by two local septs or families, the O'Flahertys on the west of the river and the O'Hallorans on the east; both were allied to the O'Connor kings. The choice of site was undoubtedly influenced by the fact that there was an important ford here, precisely at the point where the river met the sea. Turlough's fort probably was established as a focal point or frontier post, exercising control over whoever wished to cross the river. It was one of a number of such strongholds erected on his Connacht lands in the second quarter of the twelfth century. Unfortunately, it is not known where precisely the fort was situated or what it looked like, though it seems likely that it was replaced by the later Anglo-Norman castle that stood at the rear of the Custom House in Flood Street. As the only other brief references record its demolition or burning – in 1132, 1149 and 1161 – it probably consisted of some form of timber structure or stockade and clearly was capable of being rebuilt fairly quickly.

The Anglo-Norman town

Galway is not mentioned again in history until the Anglo-Norman invasion of Connacht in the early thirteenth century. Richard de Burgo, a leading Norman knight, had been granted the whole of Connacht and in 1230 came to take possession of his lands. He engaged the O'Flahertys and the O'Connors at this river-crossing and the forces faced each other on opposite sides – the Connachtmen on the west and de Burgo's army on the east. Despite some fierce fighting, de Burgo did not succeed in subduing the Irish and was forced to withdraw. He returned two years later and the annals record that he erected a castle at the mouth of the river, however this was retaken in 1233 by Felim O'Connor. Undaunted, de Burgo was back in Connacht again in 1235, this time with a much larger army, and completely subdued Felim, leaving him the O'Connor domain in Roscommon. The remainder of the lands he parcelled out among his followers, but retained the fertile plains of Galway and Mayo for his

own use. On these con-
quered lands he estab-
lished the usual manors,
villages and towns. From
then on the castle at
Galway remained firmly
under the control of the de
Burgo family and the town
which grew up around it
formed part of their principal manor of Loughrea.
Galway was established not
simply as a guard on an
important river-crossing
but was intended to be a
centre of trade in the lord-

The remains of the southeast corner of the thirteenth-
century de Burgo castle, shown under excavation in 1999.
The circular structure within the building is part of
the bowl of a later medieval limekiln.

ship, an outlet for the surpluses of the manor.

The Irish in Connacht rose out again in 1247 and the annals
mention that they 'burned the town and the castle' of Galway. This is
the first mention of the town proper, which probably consisted of
little more than a cluster of cabins and houses centred around the
castle. Although the foundation of St Nicholas's Church is generally
dated to the early fourteenth century, it may well be that a small
chapel existed here at this time to cater for the spiritual welfare of
those living in the settlement. Both castle and town were burned
again around 1266–1267, but as with earlier conflagrations no
details are recorded.

Sometime around 1270,
Richard de Burgo's son,
Walter (created earl of
Ulster in 1263), granted
his tenants a murage charter, i.e., the right to levy
tolls on a range of com-
modities (hides, fleeces,
fish, wine, salt, etc.)
coming into the settle-
ment. The monies col-
lected went to finance the

The remains of the Red Earl's hall, under excavation in 1998.

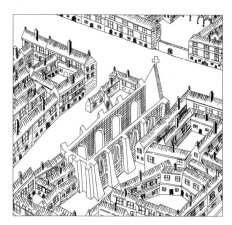

The hall, named after the Red Earl, Richard de Burgo, redrawn from the Pictorial Map of mid-seventeenth-century Galway. Richard was the son of Walter de Burgo, first earl of Ulster.

building of the town walls. Thus the process of enclosing and fortifying the town was begun, which eventually would see the area from Eyre Square to the river protected by a high stone wall. Two short stretches still survive and may be seen in the Eyre Square Centre and at the rear of the so-called Spanish Arch.

Walter de Burgo died at the castle in Galway in 1271 and was succeeded by his eldest son, Richard, known as the Red Earl (d.1326). He was the most powerful of the Norman-Irish magnates and it is most unlikely that he spent much time in Galway, his vast estates and possessions, together with his duties to two English kings, Edward I and II, keeping him otherwise preoccupied. Nonetheless, his name is linked with a large hall or residence in the town that survived until the later seventeenth century. Its foundations were recently uncovered at the rear of the Custom House in Flood Street. His first cousin, William de Burgo (d.1324), who seems to have been governing Connacht on his behalf, brought the Franciscan friars to Galway in 1296. Their foundation was established on the small island, called St Stephen's Island, outside the town to the north. Despite intermittent absences over the centuries, the friars have continued to minister to the people of Galway from this site.

Fourteenth-century Galway

Unfortunately, we know very little about the town or its development in the fourteenth century. The widespread destruction and famine that followed in the wake of the invasions of Edward Bruce (brother of the Scottish king) in 1315–1318 do not seem to have affected the citizens of Galway to any great extent. There must have been a sizeable community dwelling within the walls at this time, one that was sufficiently affluent to be able to afford a major building project at St Nicholas's Church, which was substantially enlarged around 1320.

At this period the town was very much under the control of de Burgo lords who appear to have kept a tight reign on its affairs. However, following the murder of the Red Earl's son, William, third earl of Ulster and Lord of Connacht, in 1333, things began to change. William's only offspring was an infant daughter, Elizabeth, and this left the way open for a series of struggles between various factions of the family over who should hold sway over his vast possessions. The Connacht lands were seized by two of Elizabeth's cousins, William and Eamon, sons of William de Burgo, the founder of the Franciscan friary at Galway. By 1340 Eamon controlled the lands in northern Connacht (centred on County Mayo) and his brother, William, had taken over those in the south, around County Galway. William adopted the Irish title MacWilliam Oughter (Upper MacWilliam) to distinguish him from his brother who was styled MacWilliam Eighter (Lower MacWilliam); the name de Burgo was gradually anglicised as Burke. As Galway lay firmly within MacWilliam Oughter's territory this made him, *de facto*, its lord. To what degree he was able to exercise control is unknown, but it was probably proportionate to his ability to remain head of his own faction and the limited extent to which the king's representatives in Dublin could exercise some authority in the west.

In 1348 the terrifying and devastating Black Death arrived in Ireland, brought here via the ports. The town of Dalkey, County Dublin, was one of the first places affected and within five months some 14,000 people had died in Dublin alone. Galway, being a seaport town with a developing external trade network, also must have been affected by the plague, but there is nothing on record to indicate the extent or how badly its citizens fared at this time. We may surmise, nonetheless, that its trade suffered along with the rest of Ireland, and the ensuing fifty years would be a period of recovery and development.

Although MacWilliam Oughter might claim to be lord of the town – and most of the inhabitants supported him in this – the ministers of the Crown thought otherwise. The de Burgo estates came under its guardianship in 1381 with the death of Edmund Mortimer (his son being a minor) who had inherited them through marriage (Elizabeth de Burgo having by now married and had a daughter, who married Edmund). This news was not greeted with any enthusiasm in Galway, and the exertion of the Crown's right to the Mortimer claims resulted in considerable disturbance in the town in 1385 followed by open revolt some three years later. Richard II, during his visit to Ireland in the winter of 1394–1395, pardoned the burgesses of Galway for their disloyalty, accepted the submission of MacWilliam Oughter, and pardoned and knighted him. It was probably at this time also that the grant of additional special privileges to Galway was conceived upon as a way of releasing the town from the Burke's control and attaching it to the English interest.

In November 1395 Richard granted the town a new and perpetual murage charter and in the following January gave Galway its first royal charter: this was issued in Richard II's name by Roger Mortimer (who had now come of age and was the king's lieutenant in Ireland), who was legally the lord of the town. The charter effectively raised Galway to the status of a royal borough and was an attempt to remove it from the control of the local MacWilliam lord. It was a major step forward on the road to independence for it empowered the townspeople to elect annually their own chief officer, known as a sovereign. Prior to this Galway's principal magistrate – called a provost or portreeve – had been appointed by the local lord. However, the town would not achieve full self-government, i.e., as represented by a mayor and corporation, until the end of the fifteenth century.

Among the new privileges conferred on the town was the right to exclude outsiders from any position of authority: only townspeople could trade within it, they were freed from serving on juries outside the town, and even royal officials could not lodge themselves or their retinues within the town without the townspeople's permission. Roger had included a small *proviso*, however, which specified that the lord of the town (i.e., himself) was still entitled to all the old profits and benefits. This left the citizens in a bit of a quandary for MacWilliam Oughter appears to have been claiming these, the town being within his territory. Perceiving that his power was being undermined and probably taking advantage of the fact that Roger Mortimer died in 1398, MacWilliam sacked the town in the following year. When Henry IV assumed the throne in that year he appears to have considered it expedient to placate rather than to subjugate him for, having renewed the charter to Galway in 1402, he proceeded to appoint MacWilliam Oughter as deputy for Connacht with power to enquire into Mortimer's lands in the province, and, amongst other things, to receive all the rents and profits of the town due to the king as ward of Roger's son, who was then a minor. And so, more through expediency than deliberate policy, the central Dublin administration allowed MacWilliam Oughter to exercise a hold over the town for many years.

Fifteenth-century Galway: a developing prosperity

The annals relate that Galway was burned in 1412, but neither the cause nor the extent of the damage is known. The wealth of the citizens does not appear to have been seriously affected however, and the fifteenth century may be seen as one where the merchants, realising the full potential of the town's location, developed substantial and lucrative trading links with other ports on Europe's Atlantic seaboard. Although this was an era of increasing prosperity for Galway, it is difficult to get an overall picture of its trade at this time. The staple imports were wine, iron and salt. Principal among the goods exported were hides, cloth and fish though some wool was also traded along with surplus agricultural produce. For a short period, in the mid-1370s, Galway had been licensed as one of four ports in Ireland (along with Dublin, Cork and Waterford) where merchants had to come to pay the customs due on wool. Such trade meant that the inhabitants came into frequent contact with those in its hinterland, and many merchants developed trading interests with the Gaelic

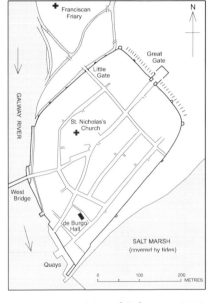

Map of Galway, c.1400.

Irish. This is best exemplified by the will, dated 1468, of one of the more prosperous Galway merchants, John Blake. Among the eighteen debtors listed, who owed him a total of 2,400 hides, there was only one foreign person, a Bristol merchant; all the rest were Gaelic Irish. Along with the sea trade, the erection of Galway's first stone bridge in 1442, which replaced an earlier structure (on the site of the present O'Brien Bridge), meant that the town was in a better position to develop its commercial contacts with those districts to the west of the River Corrib.

A half-groat (worth two pennies), coined between 1470 and 1473. The obverse side shows the head of king Edward IV and an inscription on the inner ring of the reverse side reads: VIL/LA : D/E : GAL/WAY.

Galway's growth in importance is reflected by the fact that when Edward IV assumed the throne of England in 1461 he sanctioned it, along with a number of other Irish towns, as places where the king's money could be minted. This grant was followed by a charter three years later that confirmed all existing privileges and added an important new clause: henceforth they had the right to exclude from the town anyone they chose – the lieutenant and chancellor of Ireland excepted. More especially, this right enabled them to keep out the descendants and followers of MacWilliam Burke or the Clanricards (Richard's clan named after MacWilliam's son), as they became known. But the town suffered a setback in 1473 when, as the annals relate, it 'was set on fire by lightning . . . and it would be hard to estimate the temporal wealth destroyed.' The full extent of the damage is unknown.

Independence

When the citizens came to getting their charter renewed by Richard III in 1484, they succeeded in obtaining something they had long sought: effective independence from outside control. They were now licensed to elect annually a mayor, bailiffs and corporation. In addition, even the lieutenant and the chancellor could no longer enter the town without their permission and, more significantly, the MacWilliam Burkes of Clanricard were explicitly excluded from any lordship over the town.

Running in tandem with their application for a new charter was their effort to free their local church, once and for all, from the control of outsiders. Since its foundation (sometime in the thirteenth century) St Nicholas's Church had been linked with the Cistercian monastery of Knockmoy (some twenty-seven kilometres to the northeast), whose abbot had the sole right of appointment of priests to

Galway. The citizens were not happy with this and in the 1380s successfully petitioned Pope Urban VI to establish Galway as a permanent vicarage, hoping thereby to wrestle some control from Knockmoy. But its implementation proved to be much more bothersome than anticipated, and throughout the fifteenth century there were continuous squabbles over who were the legitimate holders of the office of vicar. In fact, it is not at all certain that one Donatus O'Murray, appointed vicar in 1446, ever succeeded in filling the post. Donatus subsequently was made archbishop of Tuam and, at the request of the townspeople, set up St Nicholas's as a collegiate church while managing to persuade Knockmoy to release its jurisdiction over appointments – without, of course, jeopardising its income.

St Nicholas's Church.

An agreement to this effect was signed in Galway on 28 September 1484 and confirmed by Papal bull in February 1485. With regard to St Nicholas's revenues, the citizens, in anticipation of a successful outcome, already had bestowed on it various goods, rents and lands, and the archbishop augmented this by uniting to it the vicarage of the adjoining parish of Clare-galway. Within forty years the town corporation would succeed in annexing a further seven parishes for the church's maintenance.

Collegiate churches were quite common in England but comparatively rare in Ireland. They were organised and run in much the same way as the chapter of a cathedral church. The Galway college comprised eight priests (choral vicars) governed by a *guardianus* (anglicised as 'warden'). The archbishop took the most unusual step of giving the responsibility for the appointment of the warden and priests to the chief magistrate and freemen of the town. This was an exceptional arrangement because the archbishop effectively excluded – whether intentionally or not – his successors from the right of visitation, i.e., the official inspection of a parish by the bishop in his capacity as head of the diocese. At least, this was how the original bull came to be interpreted locally in the eighteenth century, and the ensuing disputes finally led to the dissolution of the Catholic 'wardenship' in 1831.

Certain members of the Lynch family seem to have been deeply involved in the procurement of both the new charter and the papal bull and, in particular, the brothers Pierce (Peter) and Dominick Lynch stand out as prime movers in the proceedings. Pierce Lynch was chosen as the town's first mayor on 1 August 1485 (being sworn into office on Michaelmas Day, 29 September), and his brother Dominick was elected in the following year. They were among a small number of extremely wealthy families who formed an oligarchy and controlled the town's administration. Principal among these were the Blakes, Brownes, Darcys, Frenchs, Kirwans, Lynchs and Martins. Imbued with self-confidence and civic pride, these and other merchant families proceeded to lead Galway into a century of expansion and development. This close-knit group formed alliances by marriage so that by the end of the sixteenth century many of the ruling families were related by blood, and their descendants, with a certain nostalgic hindsight, would honour them with the appellation 'Tribes of Galway'.

Despite the restrictions in the 1484 charter excluding the MacWilliam Burkes from meddling in the town's affairs, in 1504 Galway was taken by forces of the ruler of Clanricard, William Burke, as part of a long and complex struggle for power over the lands in Connacht. The king's deputy, the earl of Kildare, immediately marched westwards with a large army and on 19 August of that year defeated the Burkes and their allies at Knockdoe, some sixteen kilometres northeast of Galway. This was a decisive victory not least because it was a reassertion of the king's authority in the

The FitzGerald arms on Lynch's Castle.

west, but also because it freed the town of Galway from further encroachment by the Clanricard Burkes. The carving of the Kildare coat of arms (now on Lynch's Castle) undoubtedly must be regarded as a public acknowledgement and celebration of this victory.

Development and growth into the sixteenth century

The late fifteenth and early sixteenth century was a period of sustained growth for Galway and the town witnessed a considerable amount of building activity. The Franciscan order, which had been in residence on the north side of town since 1296, was now joined by two other mendicant orders who were invited to Galway. A Domini-can contingent arrived from Athenry in the last decade of the century and took over a small chapel belonging to the Premonstrat-ensian canons of Tuam on the west side of the river, near their present church in the Claddagh. They were followed in 1508 by the Augustinians who built a new friary on an eminence to the south of the town (present Forthill).

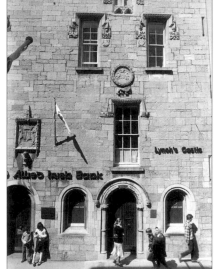

Lynch's Castle.

The fire of 1473, coupled with their enhanced municipal and ecclesiastical status, enabled merchants to erect lavish dwellings, such as Lynch's Castle. Dominick Lynch enlarged St Nicholas's Church by adding a new south aisle, a work which was completed by his son after his death in 1508. This set the tone for other families who, throughout the sixteenth century, made numerous alterations to the building. Indeed, much of the fabric that we see today dates from this period. A college house was built for the warden and vicars and it stood on the site of the present west gateway where the market is held every Saturday (the house was pulled down in the early nineteenth century).

The defences also received attention and sections of the town wall are recorded as being built (probably rebuilt) at this time. Given the increase in traffic through the port, a new or second gate was opened through the town wall onto the quays. Around 1557 a Tholsel or city hall (derived from two old English words: *toll* meaning tax and *sael* meaning hall) was commenced; it was not completed until 1580–1581. This building stood at the west end of present Main-guard Street, but it too was pulled down in the early nineteenth century. Nearly all these works were paid for by private individuals,

The Martin/Lynch plaque recording the erection of a mill and tower at the end of the West Bridge in 1562.

assisted in the case of public works by monies collected from tolls and customs. Some, however, had the assistance of State aid by way of grants of land. For example, in 1558 a Thomas Martin got a grant 'of the site of a water-mill to be built on the lower part of the bridge of Galway; provided that within two years he should build, for its defence and security, a gate of suitable height and dimensions, and a tower of stone and lime.' A stone plaque bearing a Latin inscription, now set in the premises at the junction of Shop Street and Churchyard Street, records that he fulfilled these conditions: 'Thomas Martin and Eveline Lynch caused this work and mill to be made, A.D. 1562.'

Some of the wealthier merchants also took it upon themselves to initiate individual projects to alleviate the suffering of the disadvantaged in the town. In 1505, Stephen Lynch founded a hospital or poorhouse to take care of the indigent and infirm, and in 1542 the corporation built a hospice in the east suburbs, outside the walls (on the south side of present Prospect Hill), 'as maintenance to some of the poor members of the town falling to decay'. The hospice was dedicated to St Bridget and beside it they erected a chapel. The custom soon became established that every Sunday each citizen took turns to send a servant around the town to collect alms for its support.

St Bridget's Chapel and Leper Hospital, as depicted on the Pictorial Map of mid-seventeenth-century Galway.

This hospice was subsequently used as a 'leper' hospital. There was a great fear of 'leprosy' in medieval times (a 'leper' being identified with anyone who suffered from a contagious skin disorder) and those branded lepers were never allowed to come into the town, let alone dwell in it. The Dominican church in the west suburbs also had a 'leper' house attached to it. Despite the best efforts of the authorities it was inevitable that the town would become infected with one of the epidemics that swept across Europe at this period, and in 1543 a highly contagious 'sweating sickness' is recorded as affecting Galway. The precise nature of this disease is unknown, but it was responsible for numerous deaths in the town.

Life in sixteenth-century Galway

If any word may be said to sum up the attitude of the citizens of Galway in the sixteenth century it is 'monopoly'. This was the keynote of all their trade, both at home and abroad; it was the basis of their success as merchants and the touchstone of the ruling families in the town. But this monopoly was founded on and buttressed by an English system of law and administration, and the townspeople looked to that country for culture, fashion and inspiration. Nonetheless, it was inevitable that the citizens would gradually adopt some of the customs and manners of the Gaelic Irish with whom they were in daily contact. So it should come as little surprise that many of the bye-laws passed by the corporation sought to maintain the English character of the town and its inhabitants.

The earliest dated bye-law, from the year 1460, specifically relates to the exclusion of the Gaelic Irish from the town. The corporation also forbade Irish lawyers to plead in the town's court as their system of law was completely different from that of England. In 1522 the fact that any man wishing to be elected a freeman was ordered to 'speak the English tongue and shave his upper lip weekly' clearly shows the extent that Irish was spoken in Galway at this time, even by those wealthy enough to apply for citizenship. The citizens likewise were encouraged to wear English caps and 'cloaks or gowns, coats, doublets and hose, shaped after the English fashion'. They were exhorted to send their children to school to learn

A sixteenth-century man.

to speak English and they were forbidden to partake in the Irish game of 'hurling of the little ball with hockey sticks or staves'.

All aspects of life were governed by these regulations, from the sale of the basic commodities, such as bread, meat and ale, to the discouragement of extravagant hospitality. Even gate-crashing of official banquets and parties was to be penalised, and the youths and apprentices of the town were singled out for special mention, being forbidden to play at cards and dice or partake in other 'unlawful games for money'. *Plus ça change!* The hierarchical nature of the society is reflected in the fact that 'the mayor, warden and bailiffs shall be first served with all provisions at market'; after that it was first come, first served.

It is clear that the authorities took seriously their duties regarding the public health of the inhabitants, for in 1508 it was ordered that whoever was 'found fouling the streets or walls by night or day' was to be fined, and in 1509 it was declared that 'every dweller shall make clean before his door once a week and no dung heaps be made on the streets'.

Of especial interest are the corporation's rulings on morality. In 1505 they decreed that no householder was to keep 'common whores or harlots', and a bye-law of 1519 declared that any man who 'should

be found by night time in any man's house, to give copulation, or to do with the good man's servant maid or daughter, by way of adultery' should be fined, and 'he that begets a freeman's or merchant's daughter with child shall marry her' or give her a sufficient dowry to enable her to marry another. The morals of some of the clergy must have been equally lax for in 1520 the corporation ordered that 'no priest, monk or canon nor friar shall have no whore nor lemon [an old word for *paramour*] in any man's house within this town'.

Sir John Perrott, the lord deputy, visited Galway in 1584 and was so taken aback by the apparent abuses that he initiated an official inquiry and appointed a jury of leading townspeople to examine matters. Nearly all the crafts in the town (the butchers, bakers, tailors, shoemakers, glovers) came in for criticism. Some were certainly in need of reform – the candles sold by the candlemakers, in the jury's opinion, gave 'neither light nor sight'. Not surprisingly they were also incensed by the quality of the *aquavita* (whiskey) and considered it 'ought to be called *aquamortis*' (the water of death), being more fit 'to poison the people, than comfort them in any good sort'.

The family graveslab of O'Tierney (coopers), dated 1580, in St Nicholas's Church.

The extravagant dress of some female citizens seems to have irked the more righteous members of the panel (who would have been all male), for they forbade them wear 'gorgeous apparel' and 'costly hats or cap bands of gold thread'. However, an exception was made in the case of the mayor's wife – clearly a lady with influence! Neither were women to make an 'unreasonable cry, after the Irish [fashion], either before, nor yet after, the death of any corpse' – an attempt to curb the Gaelic Irish custom of keening at wakes.

The Reformation in Galway

It is difficult to be certain when precisely the Reformation gained a foothold in the town. The earliest intimations that some inhabitants had conformed comes from the visit paid by the lord deputy in July 1538. He had come to enforce the royal supremacy, i.e., acknowledging the king as head of the Church, and this he secured from the mayor and the council. The corporation officials, as protectors of the Collegiate Church of St Nicholas, clearly saw the writing on the wall. Anticipating the dissolution of their privileges they gradually distributed to a number of citizens, for safe-keeping, some of the altar plate and furniture belonging to the church. Once this was done, they formally surrendered the church and its remaining possessions to the Crown, and at the same time petitioned for a new charter for the town and their church. But Henry VIII died in 1547 and the citizens had to wait until 1551 to obtain both of these grants

The seal of the Royal College of Galway, showing a representation of St Nicholas as bishop with three maidens kneeling for his blessing. Legend has it that he rescued these maidens from ruin by throwing three bags of money (shown on the seal to the right of the saint) in through their window.

from Edward VI, the new supreme head of the Church. Henceforth, the college would be known as The Royal College of Galway, subject, as before, to the local mayor and corporation.

In that year the lord chancellor and the master of the rolls came to Galway and went back satisfied with what they saw. Presumably the new Protestant rites were in operation and the town, both technically and legally, was now part of the Reformed Church. But the citizens were adept at walking the tightrope between the spirit and letter of the law, for the Catholic Mass continued to be publicly celebrated. And when Queen Mary assumed the throne in 1553 and re-established contact with Rome, the warden was able to assure her commissioners of the orthodoxy of the faith in Galway. However, all this was to change when Mary's sister, Elizabeth, took control in the following year. From the outset it was clear that the new queen intended to enforce acceptance of the Protestant rites, and again, anticipating a change, the warden and vicars alienated the college property so that when the Reformation was finally accepted, around 1570, little remained to support the clergy. The vast bulk of the townspeople, however, remained loyal to Rome and the Reformed college was very much a minority institution.

Internal and external forces

The sixteenth century in Ireland saw not only the introduction of the Reformation but the determined effort by the English Crown to sub-jugate the country. This involved the adoption of policies of entice-ment for those who would acknowledge the Crown as legal owner of their lands, and policies of plantation for those who would not. Some seized the opportunity to further their own ends, and in the late 1560s the sons of William Burke, the first earl of Clanricard, revolted and fought over succession rights. In the process they despoiled much of the territory around Galway. In 1572, however, they joined forces and went into open rebellion against the *cailleach grána* (the ugly hag), as they named Queen Elizabeth I. During the following decade they went on the rampage, pillaging and ransacking all before them. The town was reduced to great want as the resultant devasta-tion meant that provisions could not be brought to the Galway markets nor could the townspeople go into the countryside to trade. The *mic an Iarla* (the earl's sons), as they were known, already had razed the neighbouring town of Athenry to the ground and many in Galway were fearful that this might happen to them. The mayor was forced to ask for intervention and from time to time government troops were stationed in the town for its defence. However, by 1580 things were back to normal – or so it seemed.

In 1579 the lord justice, Sir William Pelham, described Galway as 'well built, and walled, with an excellent good haven, and is replenished with many wealthy merchants. The towns-men and women present a more civil show of life than other towns in Ireland do, and may be compared, in my judgement, next Dublin and Waterford, the only town.' On his departure he left behind a force of 100 men for its protection: this was the first permanent English garrison. The town could no longer claim to be totally separate or independent. The soldiers were an ever-present symbol of the monarch's power, a reminder that the central administration viewed some of its inhabitants with suspicion due to their long-standing trading connections with Catholic Spain – England's enemy. Considerable friction arose between the new garrison and the townspeople. In July 1583 the provost-marshal of Connacht, Barnaby Gooche, drew a map of the town showing the location for a proposed fortress or citadel (in the former Spanish Parade area), which was considered necessary to keep the townspeople in check. This is the earliest map of Galway and gives us a very good impression of the town at this time, with the houses tightly packed along the street frontages. The citadel was never built, though shortly after work was undertaken at the nearby *Ceann an Bhalla* (the head of the wall – present-day Spanish Arch), which was converted into some form of fortification.

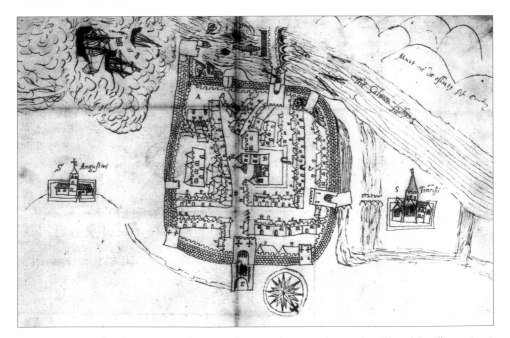

Map of Galway in 1583 by Barnaby Gooche. (North is to the right of the illustration.)

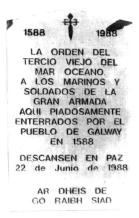

The war between England and Spain finally broke out in 1585 and three years later the fateful Armada arrived off the west coast of Ireland on its retreat homewards. One of the ships was driven into Galway Bay where, by order of the lord deputy, some 300 captured crewmen were taken to St Augustine's Church on the hill outside the town and there executed.

The 1588 Armada memorial in Forthill cemetery.

The outbreak of open war again in 1594 (the Nine Years' War) brought another period of instability for Galway. During the winter of 1596–1597 Red Hugh O'Donnell made a series of marauding raids into the south, burning all before him, and arrived at Galway in mid-January. He found the gates shut against him and the townspeople refused to sell or barter with his troops. In retaliation he burned the east suburbs and St Bridget's Hospital and Church. Although the Irish did have some successes, most notably at the Battle of the Yellow Ford in 1598, the Nine Years' War effectively came to an end with their defeat on Christmas Eve 1601 at the Battle of Kinsale.

Early seventeenth-century Galway

The opening years of the seventeenth century saw not just a new king on the throne of England (James I) but a change of attitude in Ireland. There now began to emerge a gradual identification of mutual interests among the Gaelic Irish and Anglo-Irish, or Old English as they came to be called. Though centred on religion, the bases of their interests were land and wealth, which were threatened by the rising Non-conformist parliamentarianism in England. And Galway, being very much a town inhabited by Old English families with religious (i.e., Catholic) sympathies allied to the Gaelic Irish, inevitably was drawn into this conflict.

From a military point of view the town was badly sited, for it was dominated by rising ground on the east (present Bohermore), west (present Fairhill) and south (present Forthill). While this was not especially important in its early years, it assumed a real significance after the widespread use of cannon in the sixteenth century. Eventually, it was decided that a fort should be built that would not only protect the town and its harbour but would also serve to overawe its citizens whose sympathies were seen to lie outside the realm, especially with Catholic Spain. The site chosen was the hill to the south of the town, since known as Forthill, on top of which stood the old Augustinian friary. Work began in 1602 and the fort was largely completed shortly after.

Galway was granted a new charter by James I in 1610, confirming their existing privileges and adding some significant new rights. The town was declared a separate county, distinct from the county of Galway, and its boundaries were set as being 'within the space of two miles of every part of the said town'. The Franciscan church on St Stephen's Island was excluded from this as it was designated the courthouse for the county of Galway. This new county of the town was to be governed by a mayor and two sheriffs and, as a mark of the dignity of the new office, the mayor was granted the right to have a sword borne before him on ceremonial occasions. This weapon, a large two-hander sword, survives to the present day and is still used by the corporation.

Map of the town of Galway (1610), published by John Speed in 1612.

The wealth of the citizens prospered and many chose to speculate in land and acquired substantial estates all over Connacht. We are fortunate in having a very fine description of Galway town from c.1614, which provides us with an outsider's view and this is complemented by John Speed's map of 1610.

> The town is small, but has fair and stately buildings. The fronts of the houses (towards the streets) are all of hewed stone up to the top, garnished with fair battlements in a uniform course, as if the whole town had been built upon one model. The merchants are rich, and great adventurers at sea. Their commonalty is composed of the descendants of the ancient English founders of the town, and rarely admit any new English to have freedom or education among them, and never any of the Irish. They keep good

> hospitality and are kind to strangers; and in their manner of entertainment and in fashioning and apparelling themselves and their wives they preserve most the ancient manner and state, as much as any town that I ever saw.

A fascinating insight into life under the Counter-Reformation is provided by a member of the Franciscan order, Fr Donagh Mooney, who visited Galway in 1616. At that time the Franciscan community was living secretly in a rented house in the town. He tells us that the old church and friary on St Stephen's Island to the north of the town were still preserved in very good repair as a result of the various legacies left by the townspeople. Nonetheless, as the church had been designated a courthouse some six years earlier, all the altars had been destroyed by the 'heretics': the judge's seat stood where the high altar had been. Nonetheless, on feast-days the townspeople still went there to pray. Fr Mooney relates that the man – regrettably unidentified – who had been granted possession of St Stephen's Island had passed himself off as a 'heretic', but made sure to collect all dues and legacies belonging to the monastery and these he faithfully handed over to the friars. This was a sign of the times, a period which also witnessed the State insisting on the holders of public office taking the oath of supremacy (introduced by Henry VIII) acknowledging the king as head of the Church. In Galway this led to the dismissal of four mayors who refused to take it: Oliver Brown (1610), Sir Valentine Blake (1611), Sir Peter French (1616) and Oliver Martin (1632). Matters did not improve much under James's successor, Charles I, whose policy of 'connived indulgence' towards the Catholic majority did little to redress the injustices of previous administrations. The scene was set for further change, but few could have anticipated its dramatic outcome.

The 1641 Rising and the Irish Confederation

In October 1641 the insurrection of the Catholics in Ireland broke out and heralded the beginning of a war that was to last eleven years. When the dust finally settled, in 1653, the country was devastated and the ensuing Cromwellian confiscations and transplantations resulted in the greatest change in land ownership that the country has known in its entire history.

At the beginning of the war the citizens of Galway were very much inclined to favour the insurgents, but were prevented from joining them by the presence of the English garrison in St Augustine's Fort and by the exertions of the earl of Clanricard, who had been appointed governor of the town by the king.

In October 1642 the Irish insurgents met in Kilkenny and established a government of their own, called the Supreme Council of the Irish Catholic Confederation. This body appointed a veteran soldier, Colonel John Burke, as their commander in Connacht. Burke proposed that they recapture St Augustine's Fort (in 1641 the townspeople had tried but failed to do so). After a siege lasting nine weeks the fort surrendered on 20

The remains of the Lion Tower Bastion (built 1646). It was pulled down in 1970.

June 1643. This was a day of great celebration among the Catholics in Galway and such were their joys that the Franciscans sung a High Mass in thanksgiving at their old friary outside the walls, to which they had returned. The fort was then demolished but the old Augustinian church within it was handed back to the friars. On 6 August the mayor and corporation threw open the gates and declared for the rebellion. From then until 1648, when a 'cessation' was entered into between the king's party in Ireland and the Irish Confederation, the town of Galway formed part of the insurgency movement. The decision to join the Irish Confederation would ultimately have serious consequences for the Catholic landowners of the town at the time of the Restoration.

In the meantime, the town began to prepare itself for war. The prominent position of the old St Augustine's Church remained a major concern to the military leaders and, in 1645, it too was pulled down. Aware of the town's vulnerability on its east side they built two large bastions at either end of the east curtain wall in 1646–1647.

The commemorative slab in the Franciscan graveyard, which was carved in 1645 in honour of William de Burgo, the founder of the friary.

In 1645 the Irish clergy had made it plain to the Confederation that they would not surrender any churches or property seized after 1641. A tangible expression of this commitment survives in the grave-yard of the Franciscan friary where the guardian, Fr Francis Browne, had a commemorative graveslab carved in 1645 honouring the founder of the monas-tery, William de Burgo (d.1324). As far as the friars were concerned they had returned to stay. And they were joined by other religious communities who came to seek shelter in the town: the Carmelites (1641), the Poor Clares (1642), the Capuchins (1643), the Dominican Nuns (1644) and the Augustinian Nuns (1646). The Jesuits already had a residence in Galway, having established a foundation here sometime before 1620. Catholic worship resumed in St Nicholas's Church and the college attached to it became a centre of learning during these troubled times. It was here that the famous genealogist and historian Dubhaltach Mac Fhirbhisigh (alias Duald MacFirbis, d.1671) stayed and worked on a number of manuscripts, including his celebrated *Book of Genealogies*.

In July 1649 the town was struck by a violent plague and it is estimated that some 3,700 inhabitants perished; many quitted the town and went to live in the country. It was not until the spring of 1650 that the pestilence subsided and the people gradually returned.

The siege of Galway

On the war front things had taken a turn for the worse – a large army under Oliver Cromwell landed at Dublin in August 1649. From the outset Cromwell was determined to stamp his military authority on the situation and his ensuing campaign in the east of the country was as effective as it was brutal. Word soon spread of the terror that awaited those who would not submit immediately. There was no turn-ing back now. It was all or nothing and the townspeople began preparing for a prolonged siege. They further improved their defences on the east (their most exposed side) by constructing additional bastioned works outside the old town wall.

Cromwell's Parliamentarian forces finally came before Galway in July 1651 and, to cut off all relief coming to it from the east, constructed a series of siegeworks between Lough Atalia to the south and the bogs along the Terryland River to the north. Their principal fort was at Bohermore (on the site of the present New Cemetery), and was flanked by two smaller works; a small section of the northern fort (now known as Bollingbrook Fort) still survives (see p.126 for map of fortifications and siegeworks). Fearful lest the Dominican church on the hill to the west of the town (the present Claddagh) be used as a base by the besieging army, the corporation, in agreement with the friars, pulled it down in August of that year. The siege of Galway lasted some nine months. With no relief in sight, the townspeople made the best terms they could, and on 12 April 1652 the Cromwellian soldiers took possession of the fortifications. For the citizens of Galway the war was over. The conquering army

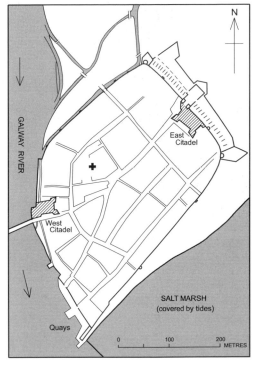

Map showing the location of the Cromwellian citadels, erected in 1652.

lost little time in making its presence felt and immediately erected two new citadels within the town – one beside the west bridge and the other blocking the main east gate. As symbols of the new social order they were built as much to house the garrison as to overawe the inhabitants.

Cromwellian Galway, 1652–1659

Dereliction and decay followed in the wake of the town's surrender. The Cromwellian soldiers did not just bring devastation by way of despoiling the buildings and churches, they also brought a 'plague', probably typhus (a fever transmitted by lice), which decimated the local population. Vast numbers of the townspeople were dispossessed and made homeless, and the military governor of Galway, Colonel Peter Stubbers, acting on orders from the government, rounded up thousands of vagrants and transported them to the West Indies where they were sold into slavery. Many clergy were imprisoned or sent overseas and the majority went into exile. At this time, according to a contemporary writer: 'you may see whole families destroyed and streets not having six families, and that soldiers or poor beggars that ought to content themselves with one cellar, had great houses to live in till they burnt all the lofts and wainscots and partitions thereof, and then remove to another house till they made an end of all the town, and left them full of excrements and filth, that it was poison to enter into any of the said houses, formerly fit to lodge kings or princes.'

The town also witnessed the more excessive elements of Puritanism. Any carvings of a devotional implication were condemned as superstition and were summarily destroyed by the soldiers. Some indication of the terror inflicted is conveyed in the following account written shortly after:

> The unruly crew broke down the coffins and monuments of the dead, and taking from them the winding sheets, as if some treasure had been within the said coffins, nay, breaking down crucifixes and such spiritual costly works engraven in fine gold ... and the monuments left wide open for the dogs to drag out and eat the corpses interred there; and likewise they erased the King's arms, and converted the church [St Nicholas's] and abbey [Franciscan friary] to stables.

And thus the centuries of wealth and almost exclusive local control ended abruptly. In 1654 the new settlers successfully petitioned the government to have the members of the corporation disenfranchised and proceeded to elect their own people as mayor and sheriffs. Their commanding officer, Peter Stubbers, was declared mayor and the soldiers of the garrison were made freemen. For the next thirty years Galway corporation was to be in the hands of the 'English and Protestants'.

The Restoration

When Charles II resumed the throne of England in 1660 the Irish Catholics expected restoration of their estates, but the Protestant interest was too firmly entrenched to be displaced. Charles owed his Crown to the Commonwealth army, and shortly after coming to the throne passed an Act of Settlement (1662) confirming the soldiers' titles to their lands in Ireland. There was a massive outcry by the Catholics and the Old English landholders, and the king attempted a compromise by passing an Act of Explanation (1665). But this only confused matters further and the claims of thousands of dispossessed and resettled Catholics were never heard. The acts reaffirmed an early declaration by the king that no one was to be restored to their lands 'who had been a member of the Irish Catholic Confederation at any time before the Peace of 1648'. The citizens of Galway now paid the price for their early support of the Confederation insurgents.

Nonetheless, the return of the monarch to the throne did bring about a certain relaxation of the more hardened Puritanical attitude to the Catholic religion, and in Galway the friars and clergy returned to minister to the people. Things had improved to such an extent that it was possible for the Dominicans to build a new chapel in 1669, on the site of their present church in the Claddagh. Within little more than a decade there were four houses in the town where Mass was publicly celebrated.

While there existed a certain tolerance of religion, there was no such leniency in civil matters for the corporation remained firmly in the control of the Protestant English settlers. But they too were facing their own problems. In 1675 the corporation found itself in a most intolerable position, with no charter or revenues available for its support as these had been declared forfeit by virtue of the town having taken part in the rebellion in the early 1640s. Charles II, with an apparent complete indifference to the general welfare of the town, granted these monies to two of his *personae gratae* at court. However, Colonel Russell, a very wealthy man and the officer in charge of the Galway garrison, came to the corporation's rescue and bought out the grantees and procured a new charter in 1677. The colonel did well from this for besides being granted all the tolls and customs, he also ensured he would be elected mayor for the succeeding years.

Pictorial Map

It was probably during the early years of Charles II's reign that the famous Pictorial Map of the town was completed. It is one of the most important historical documents that Galway possesses and presents us with a fascinating visual impression of the town at a critical juncture in its history. The map was printed in the Low Countries and is lavishly decorated in the style of the period. It is dedicated, in the most flattering terms, to King Charles II. It has been suggested that

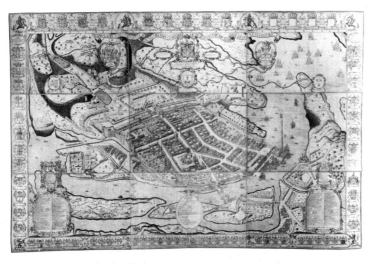

it was drawn up originally in 1651 as part of the negotiations for aid between the town and the duke of Lorraine, but there is no evidence to support this. It is not strictly a map *per se,* but, as its title informs us, an 'historical delineation'. As such, it

The Pictorial Map of mid-seventeenth-century Galway.

implies that everything illustrated is not necessarily accurately represented either in space or time. For example, the map depicts the town during the Cromwellian siege (1651–1652), but also includes St Augustine's Fort and Church, both of which had been demolished by this time. Nonetheless, it is a remarkable picture of Galway in the mid-seventeenth century and we must be grateful to its compiler, the Catholic priest Fr Henry Joyce, one-time vicar of St Nicholas's Church, for providing us with so much information on the town and its immediate environs.

We may infer from the obsequious dedication and flattering verses that this document is much more than a map: in reality, it is a piece of political lobbying. What better way to petition the King and gain his immediate attention than by presenting him with a picturesque *aide memoire* (if he needed one!) showing their town under siege by Cromwellian forces with a Royalist ship in the bay being chased by a

Parliamentarian convoy. The Catholic families of Galway (some of whom are individually named on the map) had stood by Charles through thick and thin and were now seeking redress for the hardships they had suffered: in this, as we have seen, they were to be bitterly disappointed.

The war of the two kings, 1688–1691

With the coming of Charles II's Catholic brother, James II, to the throne in 1685 conditions changed in Galway as elsewhere in the kingdom, for his accession caused a certain amount of nervousness among Irish Protestants who now feared for their land titles. In England, James's pro-Catholic policies gradually alienated his subjects and he was forced to flee to France. He was succeeded by his Protestant daughter, Mary, and her Dutch husband, William, Prince of Orange. James II was determined to recover his throne and resolved on using Ireland as a stepping stone. He landed here in March 1689 and found that most of the country – that is, the Catholic inhabitants – had remained loyal to him, refusing to recognise the new sovereigns. However, James was now faced with a dilemma: the (essentially Catholic) parliament wanted the repeal of the Acts of Settlement and Explanation in return for their support, but this would have been highly offensive to his Protestant subjects across the water. Confident of victory, the Catholics proceeded to introduce an Act of Attainder, which would result in the confiscation of almost all Protestant-held land in Ireland. And so a seed was sown that would bear fruit some years later in the imposition of the notorious Penal Laws, a Protestant retaliation that was in direct proportion to their perceived current fears.

Meanwhile, in Galway, things were progressing apace. At the outset of James's reign the Catholics in the town had supported the king and succeeded in gaining re-admittance to the corporation in 1686. Immediately, the old Protestant oligarchy was removed and the new members elected as mayor a prominent merchant, John Kirwan; he was the first Catholic to hold this office in thirty years. St Nicholas's Church was taken from the Protestants and a Catholic warden and vicars were installed. It was at this time that a new passageway was made through the town's defences on its eastern side. The old Great Gate had been blocked up by the Cromwellians when they constructed the citadel in 1652, and all traffic coming into the town had to pass through this fortress. This was troublesome and unnecessary, so a new entrance was made immediately north of the citadel. This resulted in a kink in the street at this end, one that still survives to the present day and which ultimately came to be named after the victor in the ensuing war: Williamsgate Street.

In response to a call to increase the size of James's army, six companies of soldiers were raised in Galway and, its loyalty thus confirmed, the king renewed its charter in 1688. James badly needed a military victory and was bitterly disappointed when the initial efforts of his army failed at Derry in 1689. William now sent an army to consolidate the north of Ireland and in June 1690 reluctantly came in person to supervise the war. Following his defeat at the Battle of the Boyne in July 1690 James fled to France, while William brought the war to the rest of the country before leaving Ireland at the end of the campaigning season. But the war was not over yet.

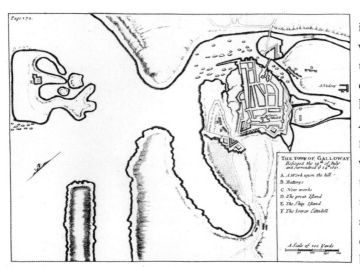

Map showing the progress of the attack on Galway, 19-21 July 1691, prepared for G Story's *History* of the Williamite war (1691).

The townspeople in Galway had been working intermittently on the fortifications since James had landed in 1689. A whole new range of fortified earthworks were constructed on the east side of the town, outside the stone-bastioned defences which had been erected in the mid-seventeeth century. Within the town opinion was divided on how to proceed. The arrival of numerous refugees after the Boyne disaster revealed the full horrors of war. There were too many people in the town by far and food was in short supply. Trade came to a standstill and many businesses closed. There was little by way of clear leadership – the town governor was found to have been in secret communication with the enemy and was summarily dismissed. It was only with the assistance of the newly arrived French soldiers and engineers, especially in the early months of 1691, that any progress was made on the town's fortifications.

In May 1691 the French general St Ruth arrived in Limerick with fresh reinforcements and the scene was now set for a major pitched battle between the two great armies. The fateful event took place on 12 July at Aughrim where St Ruth was killed and his army heavily defeated. News of this catastrophe sent shockwaves through Galway. There were calls for negotiations to be opened with the Williamites – in fact, some townspeople had already been doing just that – while others pinned their hopes on further foreign aid arriving in time to save them.

On 19 July the Williamite army appeared before the town. The defences were still incomplete and a deserter informed the approaching army that a fort on the ridge to the south of the town was not finished. Accordingly, this was the first place to be attacked and the soldiers occupying it withdrew. On the north side of the town, William's army took Terryland Castle and crossed the river: the garrison simply burned the castle and fled to Galway by boat. The taking of the fort on the hill to the southeast of the town was the deciding factor in influencing the defenders to surrender, for they knew that from here the attacking army could easily pummel the walls and fortifications with their cannon and mortars. Moreover, morale in the garrison and town was low and there was little will to continue the fight. Hostages were exchanged and after some intense negotiations Galway surrendered on 21 July. The hostilities in Ireland would drag on for another three months, but eventually would conclude with the Treaty of Limerick in October.

Medal struck to commemorate the surrender of Galway in 1691.

Eighteenth-century Galway

At the opening of the eighteenth century, Galway was a small garrison town with a population, estimated in 1706, of about 6,400 inhabitants. The majority of these were Catholics who now found themselves having to come to terms with new Protestant rulers – members of the Eyre, Gerry, Revett, Simcockes, Staunton and Wall families – who were determined to keep the town loyal to the Crown. In this they had the assistance of the infamous Penal Laws, which, from 1695 onwards, were directed specifically against Catholics. In 1703 a law was passed prohibiting any Catholic from purchasing or renting a house in Galway or Limerick. In 1717 the infamous Galway Act was placed on the statute books. Its provisions were designed to depress

The so-called Mayoralty House facing Cross Street Lower, a fine example of an early eighteenth-century house.

the Catholic majority and to ensure that a corporation subservient to the Crown should rule in the town. Henceforth, Protestants could be made freemen of the corporation without paying any fee, but as large numbers with insufficient means were thus admitted, the corporation's finances were considerably reduced as these new freemen were simply not in a position to pay the local taxes. Much of the town's trade was carried on by the Catholics, and this act had the effect of driving a good deal of it underground into smuggling, thereby further depriving the corporation of much-needed revenue. The Galway Act had its origins in a power struggle within the Protestant corporation between the more extreme anti-Catholic faction (the Whigs) and those who advocated a more tolerant treatment of the Catholic inhabitants (the Tories). The former ultimately won out and their leader, Mark Wall, was elected mayor in 1718. The new pro-Hanoverian corporation presented him with the freedom of the city in the following year.

The opening decade saw the old Cromwellian-built citadel at the West Bridge replaced by a new barrack, and a new Tholsel (begun as far back as 1639 but never finished) was completed by the corporation. This building was a potent symbol of the new social order. Among its more prominent members was Edward Eyre, whose father had acquired substantial property in and around the town. Eyre was a staunch Protestant who took his religion and politics seriously: in 1707 he objected to a candidate for sheriff on the grounds that he had a 'popish wife'.

Engraving on the lid of a seal-box accompanying the certificate of freedom of Galway, granted to Mark Wall, mayor, in 1719.

Nonetheless, he was an enthusiastic entrepreneur and endeavoured to improve the town. He built a new dock for shipping (the old Mud Dock) and laid out a roadway to it from present-day Spanish Arch (the Long Walk). Both he and his wife were generous benefactors to the poor and he also granted a piece of land to the citizens of Galway at the northern end of present Eyre Square (named after his family), which was to be kept as an open space. He was a member of parliament for the town, held the office of mayor and presented the corporation with the large ceremonial mace that is still carried before the members on special occasions today. Eyre died in 1739 (his wife, two sons and two of his five daughters having predeceased him), and was buried in St Nicholas's Church where his family memorial and that of his wife, Jane, can be seen in the south aisle.

Sketch of the Tholsel at Galway (c.1815–1820). Begun in 1639, this building was not completed until c.1709. It was pulled down in 1822.

The famine of 1740–1741

The first great potato crop failure of Irish history occurred in 1740–1741 and was the worst natural disaster of that century. It began in mid-December 1739 when a great frost spread over the whole of Ireland, which did not thaw for eight or nine weeks. The River Corrib was frozen over between Woodquay and Newcastle and the people of the town took the opportunity for some recreation and played football on it. But there was a much more serious side to this Black Frost, as it became known due to the unusual dark appearance of the ice, for it caused the entire potato crop to rot. At this time farmers had not yet begun to store potatoes in pits or clamps early in the season, instead they were usually left in the ground until Christmas. In consequence, much of the country's crop was lost. In Galway this resulted in great scarcity among the poor.

Things only got worse the following autumn. The potatoe crop again failed, and famine, with its train of calamities, crept over the land and decimated the debilitated population. A malignant fever broke out in Galway, prompting the judges to move the assizes to Tuam, but such was the fear of the disease that even the gentlemen of the county refused to attend for jury service. The town became, in the words of one commentator, 'one large lazaretto with thousands dying in the streets of famine, fever and blood flux'. To ease the situation somewhat the corporation remitted three-quarters of their market tolls in order to encourage farmers to sell at a lower rate. By the end of September things had picked up and the fever had abated, allowing some degree of normality to return to the stricken town. Fortunately, there was a marked improvement in the crop the following year, and provisions were again as plentiful as they had been scarce during the previous two years. Nonetheless, the famine and pestilence severely affected the town and the country at large, and it is estimated that in excess of 300,000 people perished. From about this period onwards the trade of the town began to decline, which, though not directly attributable to the famine, nonetheless was exacerbated by it.

Politics and Religion

One of the principal preoccupations of the Crown government in the eighteenth century was the worry that Ireland would be used as a backdoor into England by either the French or the Spanish. From time to time, on the rumour of a projected invasion, decrees would be issued ordering all suspected persons, that is Catholics, to be moved outside the town walls. On such occasions a close watch was kept on all Jacobite sympathisers. Although official policy demanded action against the local Catholic merchants, in Galway it was a case of live and let live, and as the years progressed a certain amount of tolerance of the Catholic religion was allowed. The Franciscans, Dominicans and Augustinians all had small communities in and around the town, and these were joined in 1727 by members of the Jesuit order. The reason behind the tolerance of these religious was simple: the town's trade depended on the Catholic merchants and their many relatives and correspondents in foreign countries. And though the various houses of the clergy were raided periodically to conform with the wishes of the government, there appears to have been a certain connivance practiced by the investigating officers. In the account books of the Dominican priory for the year 1730, we read that they spent two shillings and two pence on 'claret to treat the Sheriffs in their search the 11th November'.

Periodically, however, this mould was broken when a determined and spirited individual assumed power. Such was the case when Colonel Stratford Eyre (d.1767) was appointed military governor at Galway in 1747. The town was officially controlled by the corporation, but in reality the military governor had effective authority. Eyre despised the corporation, which had developed into a self-perpetuating clique. Many members were non-residents and much of their time and energy was spent carving out political niches for themselves and their friends. Eyre records disparagingly that one of the sheriffs was a shoemaker and the other a beggar. When some members came to present him with a petition about his decision to close the gates of the town early, he is reputed to have responded: 'Now gentlemen, that you are here in your corporate capacity, I must recommend to you to disperse those restless popish ecclesiastics. Let me not meet them in every corner of the streets when I walk as I have done. No sham searches, Mr. Sheriffs, as to my knowledge you have lately made. Your birds were flown, but they left you cakes and wine to entertain yourselves withal.'

Despite the prohibitions of the Penal Laws the Catholic merchants in the town prospered and by the 1730s had formed a small but cohesive middle class. And notwithstanding the disastrous famine which struck the town in the early 1740s, the number of Catholic inhabitants increased while that of their Protestant counterparts dwindled. In 1762 the population of the town and liberties of Galway had risen to 14,000. However, only 350 of these were Protestants: they were outnumbered by forty to one. In their efforts to convert some to the Protestant faith, a Charter School was established in the town. This was opened in 1755 (on the site of the present Presentation Convent, Presentation Road) and the corporation voted to donate £5 per annum by way of support. The school was little more than an orphanage or foundling hospital, as they were then called. Catholic parents were strongly discouraged from sending their children there, but the great poverty among the poorer classes in Galway meant that some were forced to allow them to attend, if only to avail of the meagre care and food provided. However, the relaxation of the Penal Laws in the late eighteenth century meant that Catholics could set up their own institutions, and in 1790 a charitable school was started in the town by the Catholic warden, supported by voluntary subscriptions. The poor no longer needed to send their children to the Charter School and so it eventually closed.

Richard Martin, 'Humanity Dick'

In the eighteenth century any perceived slight by one gentleman to another was settled by a duel, and the practice was quite commonplace in Ireland. One of the most noted duellists of the age was a Galwayman, Richard Martin (1754–1834), better known as the father of the world movement for the protection of animals. It was his friend, the future King George IV, who named him Humanity Martin, which became popularised as Humanity Dick. Martin had inherited a vast estate in Connemara, which provided him with a substantial income, and after his marriage he set up house at Dangan, on the outskirts of Galway. His cheerful and eccentric personality endeared him to all in the town, and his duelling exploits earned him the sobriquet Hair-trigger Dick. Martin was both an able lawyer and a gifted parliamentarian, and was especially noted for championing the cause for Catholic emancipation.

Both he and his wife were talented actors, and in 1782 Martin financed the building of a little playhouse in Kirwan's Lane, which opened on the evening of 8 August 1783 with a performance of two plays: 'Douglas', a tragedy that was very popular at this period, and a farce, 'All the World's a Stage'. The actors, who listed Martin and his wife in their number, were mostly members of the local Irish Volunteer corps (of which Martin was the Colonel in charge), but among them was a young twenty-year old named Theobald Wolfe Tone who would go on to play an even greater role on the wider stage of Irish history. Tone was then staying at Dangan, where he was acting as tutor to Martin's half-brothers. He became infatuated with Martin's wife who reciprocated his advances, but, as Tone recorded in his diary, without 'in a single instance overstepping the bounds of virtue'. Martin and Tone had a falling out (at this time Martin, apparently, was unaware of their affair) and the latter left Galway. Martin's interest in the theatre in Kirwan's Lane lasted only seven years because in 1790, while on a visit to Paris, his wife ran off with an Englishman. Shortly after, Martin moved from Galway and took up residence at Ballinahinch in the wilds of Connemara; he sold his interest in the little theatre in the town.

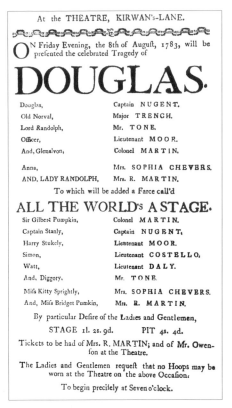

Copy of the Wolfe Tone playbill advertising the opening-night performance at Kirwan's Lane Theatre on 8 August 1783. The ladies were requested not to wear hoops, clearly a reference to the limited seating available.

Eighteenth-century Galway: the closing years

The final decade of the eighteenth century was one of turbulence in Ireland. The breakdown of the old order in France, which followed on the French Revolution in 1791, was keenly watched in Ireland where the new ideas of liberty, equality and fraternity were fast gaining ground. Many looked to that country for support, but when this finally arrived in Bantry Bay, in the winter of 1796 (with Wolfe Tone on board), it was a disaster. There was no general uprising as Tone had hoped and predicted. The French were more successful some two years later when General Humbert landed at Killala, County Mayo, at the head of an expeditionary force. This caused quite a stir in Galway, but the loyalty of its citizens was firmly on the side of the Crown. To enable the commander of the garrison to march immediately against the invading army, the merchants took up a collection and within the space of half an hour were able to present him with 1,500 guineas, a sizeable sum by any standards. The town yeomanry (the local volun- tary cavalry force) also joined forces with the garrison and both departed for the field of battle, which, as events turned out, would see them routed at Castlebar, County Mayo.

Meanwhile, Galway was left without any military presence. During the garrison's absence the Catholic clergy were to the forefront in preserving the peace. In a bizarre turn of events an Augustinian friar is recorded as standing sentinel on the West Bridge (on the site of present O'Brien Bridge), a place where but a few decades earlier he would have been apprehended and imprisoned.

Later in the year another French expedition sailed into Lough Swilly but was captured, yielding up none other than Wolfe Tone. Imprisoned in Dublin, Tone evaded the hangman's noose by playing for real a part he had once acted so well on the stage in Galway some fifteen years earlier: he committed suicide. And so with the defeat of the French in Ireland, Bonaparte's hoped-for little diversion came to an end.

Curiously, it was during the last decade or so of the eighteenth century that things began to pick up in Galway. By this time the infa- mous Penal Laws had been substantially removed from the statute books and the future looked bright for the Catholic merchants. Such optimism is reflected in their increased efforts to improve the town. Some of the old town walls and fortifications were pulled down and warehouses erected in their place. The increase in commerce also brought an increase in population as many were attracted to the town by prospects of employment. At the opening of the new century there were estimated to be at least 20,000 inhabitants in Galway – almost three times that of the early 1700s. The poor crowded into many of the old houses in the town and suburbs, living in squalid and unsanitary conditions. The commercial and landed classes began to move out and build new houses for themselves along the fashionable Dominick Street, around Meyrick (later Eyre) Square and in the more salubrious east and west suburbs.

One of the curious aspects of the development of Galway in the eighteenth century was the manner in which the small fishing village on the west side of the river, at the Claddagh, had evolved into a tightly-knit community. Differing in language, laws and customs from their neighbours across the river, they would become the special focus of numerous travel writers and visitors in pre-Famine times. Their story would come to reflect that of the town itself in the nineteenth century, a tale of expansion followed by inevitable decline (see The Claddagh in part two).

An early nineteenth-century house, Dominick Street.

Nineteenth-century expansion

Galway assumed the role of service centre for the entire province during the opening decades of the century and the town experienced a mini-building boom. In 1801 the commanding officer in Galway, General Meyrick, enclosed the Green (present Eyre Square) as a parade ground for soldiers, and also widened the old West Bridge to accommodate the increase in traffic from the west suburbs and beyond. Within the town some of the older houses were renovated, including Lynch's Castle, which was extensively remodelled into its present form. A new Custom House was built in Flood Street and the sixteenth-century Tholsel in Mainguard Street (in use as a military guardhouse and town jail) together with its replacement, the new Tholsel in Shop Street (in use since 1709), were pulled down and the streets widened. Increased State involvement in the lives of the people was marked by the building of two new jails for the town and county on Nuns' Island, and new courthouses opposite them in Newtownsmith. To facilitate the journey from conviction to incarceration

The county courthouse, built 1812–1815.

the respective establishments were linked by a brand new bridge, the present Salmon Weir Bridge.

Efforts were made to clean up the town in 1802 and a new spacious County Infirmary was opened at Prospect Hill, on the site of the former County Buildings. Among the major contributors to the malodorous state of affairs were the butchers and fishmongers: the latter, in particular, seem to have had little regard for public health. To help improve matters a fish market was erected at the quays in 1800, and two years later an extensive meat market was built in Williamsgate Street (on the site of present Corbett Court shopping centre). Before this the butchers had exhibited their wares on various streets around the town, though principally at the barracks beside the West Bridge,

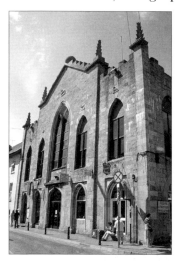

The former St Nicholas's Parish Church (1816-1821), Middle Street, which served as the Pro-Cathedral from 1831 until 1965.

which, in consequence, became known as the Shambles Barracks. But old habits die hard and it was necessary to call in the military to compel them to use the new meat market.

The developing religious toleration that was a feature of Ireland under the Union was well illustrated in Galway, where, in 1816, the laying of the foundation stone of the new Catholic parish chapel in Middle Street was presided over by the Protestant mayor with numerous other Protestants in attendance. Completed in 1821, it became the Pro-Cathedral on the establishment of the Catholic diocese of Galway in 1831. Although the clergy of both denominations were particularly active in Galway during the initial decades, especially in establishing charitable institutions for the poor, the large Catholic population was now served by an increasing number of churches and religious. In 1815 the

Dominicans opened a new chapel in the Claddagh and the Presentation nuns established a convent in Galway. They subsequently took
over the old Charter School premises, which had been used as a barrack between 1798 and 1814; they reside there still. Another barrack
building, in Lombard Street, was taken over by the Patrician Brothers who came to Galway in 1827. The establishment of these teach-
ing orders foreshadowed that of the State, which introduced its own
elementary education system in 1831 and subsequently favoured
Galway as the location for one of its three new Irish universities in
1845.

Industry and commerce

The driving force behind the mini-industrial revolution in Galway in
the first half of the nineteenth century was water. This is what pow-
ered almost forty mills in and around the town – breweries, distiller-
ies, flour mills, oat mills, malt mills, tuck mills, saw mills (for wood
and stone), a paper mill and a bleach mill. Agriculture was very much
the basis of the local economy, while the main imports included coal,
hemp, iron, tallow, timber, salt and wine. Numerous warehouses and
stores sprang up, especially in the Merchants' Road and Back Street

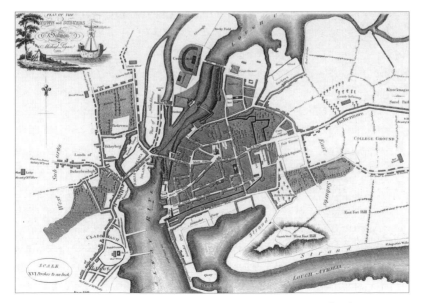

Logan's map of Galway (1818)
prepared for Hardiman's *History of Galway* (1820).

(present St Augustine Street) areas. All gave employment and the population increased as many were attracted from the countryside to work in the mills and stores. But such a huge mass of labour meant that wages were pitifully low and the living conditions of the majority of the workers was deplorable. The improved commercial ambience is reflected in the formation of a small number of private banks (or discount houses as they were called) though one of these, run by John Joyce (*d*.1818), collapsed, causing considerable hardship. By the 1830s their place had been taken by branches of the Bank of Ireland and Provincial Bank.

A post-bill from the bank of M&P Lynch, one of a number of local banks operating in Galway in the early nineteenth century.

Efforts to improve the port facilities were undertaken firstly on the west side of the river, at the Claddagh, where there was a large fishing fleet. New quays were built there and these were followed in 1822 by Nimmo's Pier (named after the famous Scottish engineer Alexander Nimmo, who oversaw numerous public works in the west of Ireland). The lighthouse on Mutton Island came into operation in 1817 and greatly facilitated navigation. Plans had long been afoot for a new docks at Galway to replace the existing ones in front of the Spanish Arch, which were old and unsuited to the larger vessels now coming to the town. In 1830 a Galway Harbour Board was established and three years later, with the aid of a government loan, work began on the construction of new docks, which were completed in 1842. In tandem with the development of the port area the grand scheme had always envisaged the opening up of all the inland water systems of Loughs Corrib and Mask, which would allow produce from those areas to be brought by boat to the town port. In 1820 Nimmo had suggested cutting a canal on the east side of the town to link Woodquay with the proposed docks, but this scheme was rejected in favour of the canal being located on the west side of the town. Work began on this project in 1848 and it was officially opened four years later.

The most serious threat that faced Ireland in the early nineteenth century was the extent to which its population was dependant on one single crop: the potato. When shortages occurred, as they did all

View of the old West Bridge and Fish Market areas, from WH Bartlett's *The Scenery and Antiquities of Ireland* (1842).

along the western seaboard in the early decades of the century, havoc ensued in Galway as large numbers of poverty-stricken people flooded in from the surrounding countryside, especially from Conne-mara. The typhus epidemic that swept across Ireland between 1817 and 1819 (caused by the poor harvests of 1816–1817) first appeared in Galway in 1816 and lasted almost two years. As a result of this a fever hospital was built to the north of the town on Earl's Island in 1820 (the present Irish Centre for Human Rights, NUI Galway). This hospital saw intense service during the famine and fever that struck two years later. But Galway did recover and, despite an out-break of cholera in 1832, it continued to expand and develop.

By the early 1840s a certain air of pros-perity permeated the town. It had recently been lighted with gas (1837), a chamber of commerce had been incorporated under the title of the Royal Galway Institution (1839), Eyre Square had just been enclosed with

The former St Patrick's Parish Church. It ceased to be a church in 1972.

railings giving the area a quasi-Georgian appearance, St Nicholas's Church had been reopened after a complete refurbishment, new churches and meeting houses had made their appearance (Franciscans at Newtownsmith; St Patrick's parish church, Forster Street; Methodists, Queen Street; Presbyterians at Nuns' Island), the extensive docks were completed and plans were afoot to start a major drainage and navigation scheme. This sense of optimism and well-being was captured by William Makepeace Thackeray, who visited Galway in 1842 and wrote: 'Great warehouses and mills rise up by the stream, or in the midst of unfinished streets here and there, and handsome convents with their gardens, justice-house, barracks, and hospitals adorn the large, poor, bustling, rough-and-ready town.'

Famine and decline

The air of prosperity noticed by Thackeray was not to last. Between 1845 and 1849 Ireland was gripped by the dreadful Great Famine, which caused widespread death, destitution and destruction and which irreversibly transformed the demography of the whole country. It took a heavy toll on Galway as the hungry destitutes crowded into the town seeking work and sustenance. Although relief was provided by way of public works (on various road schemes, the building of the university and the drainage and canal projects in particular), these were hopelessly overloaded. Threadneedle Road in Salthill was built at this time and its Irish name, Bóthar na Mine (the road of the meal), recalls that those working on it were paid in Indian meal. The Galway workhouse, built in 1840–1841 to accommodate 800 inmates, was forced to house as many as 1,300 by November 1847, and it became necessary to establish auxiliary workhouses in and around the town. The county jail, which, prior to the Famine, had averaged sixty-eight inmates per year, now housed between 650 and 750; it was designed to hold 110. A Breakfast Institute had been established by the Patrician Brother Paul O'Connor in 1830 to help the hundreds of boys attending his school in Lombard Street (the 'Old Mon', i.e., monastery, as it later became affectionately known) and it played a crucial role during these years, often providing the only daily meal for at least 1,000 children. In 1848 one commentator recorded that 'in Galway 3,000 starving beggars roamed the streets, with the children mere animated skeletons screaming for food'. As mortality figures soared the only hope of survival for many lay in emigration; Galway's greatest export at this period was its people. The town did not recover from this severe blow and the population, which had stood at over 20,500 in 1851, continued in a slow decline throughout the remainder of the century until there were less than 13,500 people recorded in the 1901 census for the municipal borough.

Most of the public works undertaken in the first half of the century were supported either by local initiatives or by State subsidy, the corporation by this time having largely become inefficient and inadequate. It was officially abolished in 1841; it had been replaced some years earlier by a body of twenty-four town commissioners who took a more pro-active role in developing the town. Chief among its members were the Catholic priest Fr Peter Daly (d.1868), and the Protestant vicar of St Nicholas's Church, Rev. John D'Arcy (d.1875). Both were united in their concern for the people and the development of Galway, and they sat on almost every important committee or board in the town.

Of the two, Fr Daly was the more controversial and colourful figure. Intelligent, headstrong, ambitious and endowed with great energy, he became directly involved in every major project in the town. As a member of the Harbour Commissioners he sought to establish Galway as a transatlantic port. He was responsible for the introduction of the newly established order of nuns, the Sisters of Mercy, to the town in 1840, and as chairman of Galway Town Council he was a member of the delegation that went to 10 Downing Street in 1852 to lobby for improved harbour facilities. There were many who supported him in Galway, and at times this irked his ecclesiastical superiors who strongly disapproved of his

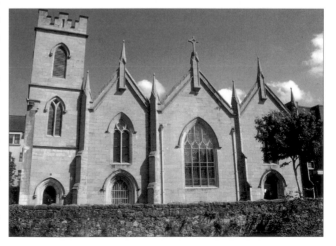

The chapel of the Sisters of Mercy convent, Newtownsmith, which for many years was known as Fr Daly's Chapel in honour of the Catholic priest who was instrumental in bringing the order to Galway.

The official opening of the canal,
28 August 1852, by the duke of Eglinton,
after whom it was named.

meddling in local politics. Notwith-standing their admonitions, Fr Daly refused to change his ways. During the Great Famine he ran soup kitchens and even gave over his own residence, Albino Lodge on the Galway–Moycul-len road, for the relief of the destitute. The only visible evidence of his former presence in the town are the little street known as Daly's Place (at the junction of Woodquay and Francis Street – renamed in 1858 in his honour by his fellow town commission-ers) and the chapel attached to the Convent of Mercy, which for many years bore his name.

The Great Famine alone cannot be blamed for the economic slug-gishness that seemed to overcome the town in the second half of the nineteenth century. The coming of the railway to Galway in 1851 opened up the west to a whole range of manufacturers and distribu-tors in Dublin, and the local industries faced growing competition from cheaper imports. Rather than days it now took only hours by train to reach Galway from Dublin. The initial success of the newly completed canal – opened with great pomp and ceremony by the

The first Claddagh Bridge (built 1850). This was replaced by an iron one in 1887, which was superseded by the present concrete structure in 1934.

duke of Eglinton in 1852 (after whom it was named) – did not last for long as the railway greatly impacted on its development. The building of the canal, however, was only one part of a much broader plan for the whole river system of the town. When all the works were finally finished in the mid-1850s, Galway not only had a canal, tidal basin, regulating weir and extensively refurbished river and mill-race system, but also two new bridges: the old West Bridge was replaced with a new stone one (the present O'Brien Bridge) and a wooden bridge linked the Claddagh with the Fish Market.

Several attempts were made to promote Galway as a transatlantic port, especially in the 1850s and early 1860s. Indeed, the Midland and Great Western Railway Company had been quite confident that this would happen, hence the extraordinary size of their Railway Hotel. The Atlantic Steam Navigation Company – better known as the Galway Line – was established in association with a Manchester businessman, John Orwell Lever, and it was hoped that Galway might

A Galway tram heading up Shop Street.

be made the eastern terminus of the Atlantic mail service. Unfortunately, these schemes were unsuccessful and floundered – as did some of their ships. Despite poor economic growth further improvements were made to the town, and by the late 1860s it had a comprehensive piped-water supply and, by 1880, an extensive sewerage system. The new docks (enlarged by the addition of a deeper berth, the Dún Aengus Dock, in 1881–1883) and railway terminus ensured that Galway still maintained its strategic position as the centre of commerce and distribution for the western region, yet it did so not with any great sense of drive or determinism but with a general phlegmatic air of resignation. Most visitors to the town at this time saw Galway as a run-down, provincial centre. Indeed, its only real import of any consequence were the tourists who now came by railway to enjoy the wonderful scenery in Connemara and the Aran Islands or to bathe at the developing seaside resort at Salthill, which had begun to re-establish itself around the middle of the century. Indeed, so popular had Salthill become that a tramway was opened in 1879 linking it to the railway station. In the following year the Canadian-based Allan Shipping Line began scheduled sailings between Galway and America, which lasted until 1905. Although the ships brought much-needed revenue and life to the port, they also provided the means whereby thousands of emigrants left the west of Ireland for a new life in a new world.

A provincial town

The opening of the Galway–Clifden railway line in 1895 marked another determined effort to open up the west and to develop the fisheries and other local industries. By the opening of the twentieth century scarcely any of the industries that were established in the town during its earlier mini-industrial revolution had survived. Nonetheless, it could boast of having its own electricity supply (established 1898) and the town celebrated with style the brief visit of the king of England, Edward VII, and his queen in June 1903. It also

RAILWAY VIADUCT. GALWAY 6805-W.L.

hosted its own Great Exhibition in 1908 to stimulate economic growth. But despite the efforts of some enterprising merchants and businessmen, Galway could not shake off the weight of decay that seemed to permeate many of the older buildings. As one visitor put it:

The railway viaduct over the River Corrib. It had a central bridge that could be raised to allow sailing craft pass through.

'Galway bears upon its face a readable proclamation of having seen better days. It is dirty, unkempt, badly paved, most indifferently lighted, and the houses dilapidated and depressing. Vacant warehouses and dwelling-houses – I saw rows, regular streets of them – seem more in number than the occupied. The whole town has a depressing effect.' In 1911 the population was 13,266, its lowest in well over 100 years.

With the outbreak of the First World War in 1914 a massive recruiting campaign was organised in the west by the local Connaught Rangers, who were stationed at Renmore Barracks, and many Galwaymen went off to war never to return. Horses were requisitioned and the local tram company in the town suffered as a result. The financial difficulties which brought about its closure in 1918 were caused as much by the war as by the development in petrol-driven vehicles. From its ashes rose the new Galway General Omnibus Company in 1919.

Medal struck to commemorate the Great Exhibition in 1908.

The 'Troubles' and Civil War

The Easter Rising of 1916 made little impact on the town. A few brief engagements took place to the east under the command of Liam Mellowes, whose statue now graces the esplanade at the top of Eyre Square. The years 1918–1921, or as they are often called the 'Troubles', were turbulent years in Ireland. In Galway a number of buildings were commandeered to house various auxiliary units, which had been brought in to stem the activities of the local IRA. These were augmented by the notorious Black and Tans whose ruthlessness only served to fuel the flames of discontent. On 19 October 1920 the Black and Tans took local Sinn Féin urban councillor Michael Walsh from his home and shot him – a plaque on the Long Walk marks the spot where his body was thrown into the river. A local curate, Fr Michael Griffin, suffered a similar fate almost a month later. Both subsequently were honoured by having streets named after them: Walsh's Terrace, Woodquay (1924) and Fr Griffin Road (1937).

Following the signing of the Anglo-Irish Treaty in December 1921, the evacuation of all British military personnel began. In February 1922 they marched out of Renmore Barracks and handed it over to the local battalion of the IRA. But the Treaty was not accepted by all republicans, and in Galway people were divided between pro- and anti-Treaty sympathisers. The differing factions commandeered various buildings in the town, but after some sporadic fighting the anti-Treaty forces were obliged to quit their positions, leaving the pro-Treaty forces in control.

The emerging capital

Although the population of the county continued to decline in the 1920s and 1930s, in the city it rose and this placed a severe strain on housing. In consequence, extensive public housing schemes were initiated by the urban council, especially in the Bohermore and Claddagh areas. The bulk of the old Claddagh village disappeared at this time and was replaced by terraced houses. Galway, with its particularly strong Irish-speaking hinterland, was ideally placed when the language was revived as the official vernacular. An Irish-speaking battalion was stationed at Renmore Barracks in 1925 (renamed Dún Uí Maoilíosa, Mellowes's Fort, in 1952 after the local leader of the 1916 Rising), a dedicated Irish-language theatre, An Taibhdhearc, opened its doors in 1928 and an all-Irish primary school, Scoil Fhursa, was established in 1931. The new Irish government also stipulated that

Summer at Salthill.

Headed bill of O'Gorman's Bookshop and Printing House,
Shop Street (now Easons).

an increasing proportion of the academic and administrative functions of the university were to be performed through the medium of
Irish.

One of the landmark developments in Galway's economic history
was the formation – in reality, a reformation – of the chamber of commerce in 1923. This body was at the forefront in re-establishing the
city as a transatlantic port. The first liners arrived in 1927, two years
later over seventy ships had called there and by 1933 this had risen to
over 100. In consequence, there was a growth in tourism, both in the
seaside suburb of Salthill and in the town itself. However, all this
would cease with the outbreak of the Second World War.

Some success was achieved in the setting up of a number of industries in Galway at this time, though the economic climate of the
1930s saw the closure of the Galway–Clifden railway in 1935; the
large metal bridge spanning the River Corrib was sold as scrap for
£10. The old jails on Nuns' Island were closed in 1939, and two years
later the county council handed them over to Bishop Michael Browne
as the site for his proposed cathedral. Efforts had been ongoing to
re-establish the old corporation (abolished in 1841), and in 1937 an
act was passed instituting Galway as a borough with a mayor, alder-
men and burgesses. The first mayor was a leading businessman,
Joseph F Costelloe, who continued to be elected to this office until
his retirement in 1950. He holds the singular distinction of being the
longest-serving mayor in the entire history of the corporation.

The 'Emergency'

The outbreak of the Second World War – or the 'Emergency' as it was euphemistically referred to in Ireland – came suddenly to Galway. On the very first day of the war (3 September 1939) the townspeople were called on to help one of its very first casualties: the survivors of the passenger ship *Athenia*, which had been fleeing the impending war in Europe with over 2,000 passengers on board. It was sunk by a German U-boat in the Atlantic to the northwest of Ireland. One of the two rescue ships signalled that it intended to land the survivors at Galway. Immediately, the hospitals in Galway were put on alert to receive the sick and wounded, and many hotels and private individuals put their premises at the disposal of the survivors. All were well looked after until such time as they were ready to leave.

The awakening city: 1950 onwards

In Ireland, the decade after the Second World War was a period of economic stagnation and a general mood of despondency prevailed over the country. There was massive emigration, rising unemployment and a declining population. The protectionist policies of the 1930s had not worked and there was little by way of industrial development: agriculture was still the basis of economic activity. In 1958 the government published the Programme for Economic Expansion (the first of three such programmes), which was a major departure in policy. This favoured an abandonment of self-sufficiency in favour of the development of free trade with an emphasis on exports and the attraction of foreign investment. Galway had already anticipated this by a number of years – in 1953 the chamber of commerce had established an investment trust company and raised some £15,000. This was used to help start the Royal Tara China company in Mervue, the first of many major industries to be established on this side of the city.

Despite the economic difficulties of the 1950s all was not doom and gloom in the town, and steady progress was made in the areas of tourism, healthcare, housing and education. Salthill benefited not just from foreign tourists but also from the emerging middle classes throughout the country who came here in increasing numbers on holiday. In 1952 Merlin Park Hospital opened its doors as a

Galway from the air (mid-1950s). Note the site of the former Galway county jail,
now occupied by the Cathedral and car park.

sanatorium to combat one of the great health scourges of the time,
tuberculosis, and the long-anticipated Regional Hospital (now University College Hospital) was opened in 1956 on the site of the old
workhouse. A major housing scheme was built in the early years of
the decade to the west side of the city, at Shantallow, and in 1954 the
Patrician Brothers opened a substantial new primary school on the
site of the old Shambles Barracks. The Eglinton Canal, then deemed
obsolete, was closed to traffic and its swivel bridges were replaced by
permanent concrete ones. The crowning event of the decade took
place on 27 October 1957 when Cardinal D'Alton, Archbishop of
Armagh and Primate of All Ireland, blessed the site and foundation
stone of the new Catholic cathedral in the presence of a large gather-
ing, which included the President of Ireland, Seán T Ó Ceallaigh, and
the Taoiseach, Eamon de Valera.

The 1960s in Galway, no less than the country as a whole, were
characterised by a social dynamic that saw considerable change in all
walks of life and heralded a spectacular phase of growth that continues to the present day. The triumphant visit of President John F

The blessing of the foundation stone for Galway cathedral in 1957 by Cardinal D'Alton.

Kennedy to the city in June 1963 symbolised for many the outward-looking face of the changing Ireland. There was a general shift in government policy towards the development of regional centres for new industries and Galway was well positioned to capitalise on this initiative. The chamber of commerce had already bought land at Mervue with the intention of enticing industries, and this was sold to the State-run Industrial Development Authority (IDA): thus was born Galway's first industrial estate, which opened in 1967. The drive to modernise Irish industry also resulted in the formation of a series of third-level education institutions (Regional Technical Colleges) and the Galway RTC opened its doors in 1972 (since 1998, the Galway–Mayo Institute of Technology). Although there was something of a down-turn in growth when the international economic climate turned sour in the late 1970s, the visit of Pope John Paul II to Galway on 30 September 1979 provided a much-needed boost to morale and was celebrated with great enthusiasm and verve: some 300,000 people attended his special youth mass at Ballybrit Racecourse.

Urban renewal

The quincentenial celebrations of 1984 – commemorating the formal establishment of Galway corporation 500 years earlier – witnessed a re-awakening of pride in the city. This momentum received a special boost two years later when Galway was established as a county borough, resulting in substantial changes to its boundary. In the same year the city was granted special urban renewal tax concessions under the Designated Area Scheme and this resulted in major developments in the Merchants' Road and docks areas. Since then the city has been completely revitalised. A network of new approach roads, roundabouts, a new bridge (Quincentenary Bridge), several new housing developments, multi-storey car parks, hotels, restaurants, shopping centres and residential apartment blocks have appeared, almost as if overnight. Never in its history has the city witnessed so much building and development.

In an effort to preserve some of the character of the older city, the historic centre has been pedestrianised and paved, the Fish Market and Courthouse Square areas have been landscaped and a riverside walk, Bruach na Coiribe, has been opened to link Wolfe Tone Bridge with Newtownsmith. The old historic town continues to exercise a degree of influence over the direction in which the modern city is moving, and there is much enlightenment in the works now being undertaken to improve the city. The founding of Galway Civic Trust (Dúchas na Gaillimhe) in 1992 and the appointment of an Arts Officer (1990) and Heritage Officer (1999) within the corporation is a reflection of the greater awareness of these issues at local level.

A restored nineteenth-century warehouse, Abbeygate Street Lower.

The last four decades of the twentieth century saw the fortunes of Galway steadily improve. It has grown at a faster rate than any other Irish town, from a population of nearly 24,000 in 1961 to almost 51,000 in 1991, displacing Limerick, in 1996, as the third largest urban centre in the State, with a population of 57,241. These decades have seen the construction of large housing estates along the principal road networks approaching the city, at Newcastle on the west and Mervue, Renmore and Terryland on the east, with an almost continuous ribbon development westwards along the coast road to Barna.

The living city and heart of the west

But what of Galway today? There is a youthful exuberance and bustle about the city that marks it out as a modern Mecca of the arts, where students, tourists and locals meet in quaint pubs and restaurants amid the hustle and bustle of the busy, working city. The student populations from both the university and the Institute of Technology have done much to revitalise the boom in creative arts, most notably in the world of theatre, where the internationally renowned Druid Theatre Company (founded in 1975) has been a landmark success. Located on the edge of the great Connemara Gaeltacht, Galway also has become, in essence, the Gaelic capital of Ireland. It prides itself on being the centre of Gaelic culture and learning and the Irish language can be heard on its streets.

A new Galway skyline emerges above the John F Kennedy Memorial Park, Eyre Square.

Galway is probably best known for its busy social calendar of festivals. Among the many highlights is the Jazz Festival (February), followed by the Cúirt International Poetry Festival (April). The city really comes alive during the summer months with the Galway Film Fleadh and the Galway Arts Festival, the city's annual feast of fun, which has become one of the foremost events in the Irish calendar. There is a huge emphasis on taking the festival into the streets, and the Galway-based Macnas troupe are one of its main attractions. For race-lovers there is the famous Galway Races, held at the end of July

The Galway-based Macnas troupe performing
at the Galway Oyster Festival.

and one of the sporting highlights of the racing year, and all tastes
and palates are catered for at the Galway International Oyster Festival in late September. And there are many other festivals and events
held in different localities all around the city, each contributing to
the celebration that is Galway today.

Inevitably, with all the talk surrounding that major landmark in
time, the millennium,
Galway finds itself look-
ing backward and for-
ward. History tells us that
there has always been a
tension between past and
present, between conti-
nuity and change,
between tradition and
innovation. This is the
challenge that has faced
the citizens of Galway

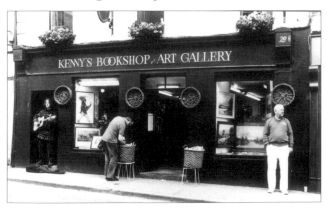

Busking in High Street, outside Kenny's Bookshop.

from earliest times and one that will continue into the future. None-theless, the city is better placed than ever before to cope with this change, for Galway symbolises the potency of the new Ireland at the dawn of a new century, a vibrant centre embracing both the traditional and the modern. This is its hallmark and one which – for both visitor and native alike – makes it the most rewarding of Irish capitals.

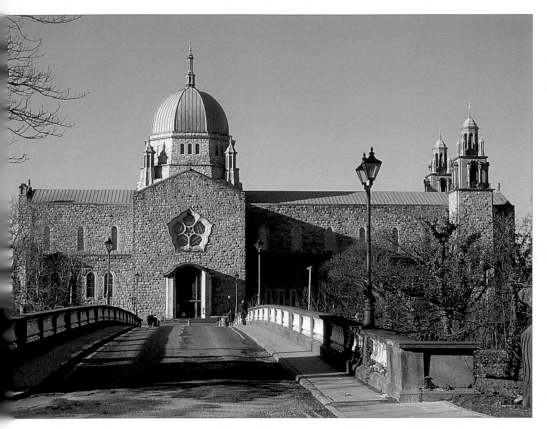

Above: Galway's most outstanding public monument of the twentieth century: the Cathedral of Our Lady Assumed into Heaven and St Nicholas (1958–1965).

Right: Looking towards the high altar, under the crossing, with the impressive mosaic of the Crucifixion on the south gable beyond.

Below: This leaping salmon at the Salmon Weir Bridge rises from the stump of one of the great elms that formerly graced the riverbank.

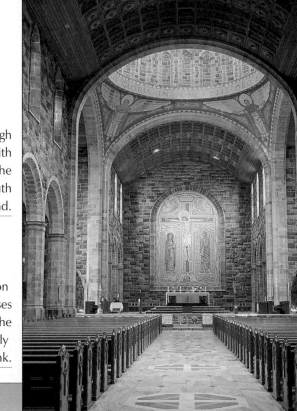

Looking north along the River Corrib, towards William O'Brien Bridge, from the riverside walk *Bruach na Coiribe* (the bank of the Corrib).

restored Fisheries Watch Tower (1853) at Wolfe Tone Bridge, now a small fisheries museum.

Above: The Fish Market area where the old medieval quays (now covered over) were situated.

Left: The restored Blake's Castle, Quay Street.

Above: A section of the old town wall at the rear of the so-called Spanish Arch.

Left: The well-known 'Seaġan Ua Neaċtain' pub at the corner of Cross Street and Quay Street. The building probably dates to the late sixteenth or earlier seventeenth century. It reputedly was owned by Colonel Richard Martin (1754–1834), otherwise known as Humanity Dick (one of the founders of the Royal Society for the Prevention of Cruelty to Animals in 1824), and also as Hair-Trigger Dick because of his readiness for duelling.

Top of opposite page: The busy Saturday market outside St Nicholas's Church.

Left: The Quincentenial Fountain, Eyre Square: a popular rendezvous that picks up Galway's nautical associations.

Below: St Augustine's Well on the seashore at Lough Atalia.

Right: The baptismal font in St Nicholas's Church, dating from the late sixteenth/early seventeenth century. The carved tracery on its side echoes that of the windows in the north aisle.

Right: The colourful blue and yellow tiles with the monogram of the name Jesus (IHS) surrounded by flaming rays. This emblem was used by St Bernardine of Sienna (*d*.1444) who preached that the Holy Name should be placed above the doorways of houses. The practice was revived in the 1920s throughout the towns and cities in Ireland where the Franciscan order had houses.

Above: Part of the old town wall in the Eyre Square Centre, with the reconstructed corner tower.

Left: The postbox at the corner of High Street and Mainguard Street. Designed by GW Penfold in 1865, it bears the intertwined initials of Queen Victoria (VR – *Victoria Regina*).

Queen's College, Galway, built 1846–1849, now part of the National University of Ireland.

Bringing cool elegance to the modern NUI Galway campus: the Martin Ryan Marine Science Institute. The clock on the pediment above the entrance mirrors that in the tower of the original nineteenth-century building (the 'Quad') directly opposite.

Left: Lynch's Castle on the corner of Shop Street and Abbeygate Street Upper, at the heart of the old medieval town.

Below left: A fragment of old Galway stonework, High Street. This keystone from a fireplace is dated 1615 and carved with the arms of the Frenchs and Fonts, two of Galway's 'tribal' families.

A moment of quiet at Eyre Square beside the statue of one of Ireland's most famous writers in the Irish language, Pádraic Ó Conaire (*d.*1928).

Summertime in the John F Kennedy Memorial Park, Eyre Square.

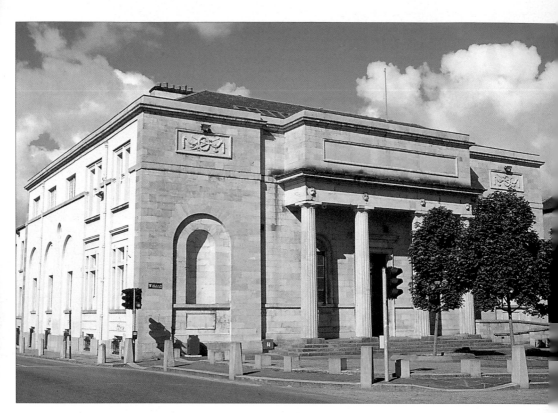

Galway county courthouse, designed by Richard Morrison and opened in 1815.

A charming representation of the English (Hanovarian) royal arms that formerly graced the top the portico of the courthouse. It now stands in the grounds of the university.

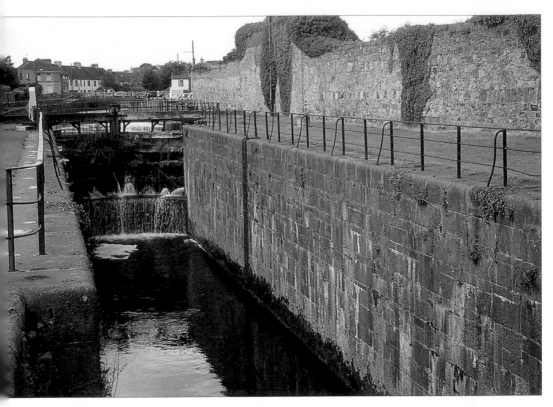

The principal lock on the mid-nineteenth-century Eglinton Canal at Parkavera
(Páirc an Mhéara – the mayor's field) near Dominick Street.

Live entertainment in William Street.

A rare example of fine Georgian architecture in Galway. The so-called Mayoralty House, Flood Street, dates from the early eighteenth century.

A tasteful blend of the old and new at the corner of Forster Street and Frenchville Lane.

Above: Kirwan's Lane: Galway's 'Left Bank'.

Left: A view down Kirwan's Lane where Richard 'Humanity Dick' Martin had a little theatre in the 1780s.

Quay Street, which would once have led to the busy medieval quays in front of the Spanish Arch, is still one of Galway's liveliest thoroughfares.

A GUIDE TO THE
HISTORIC CITY

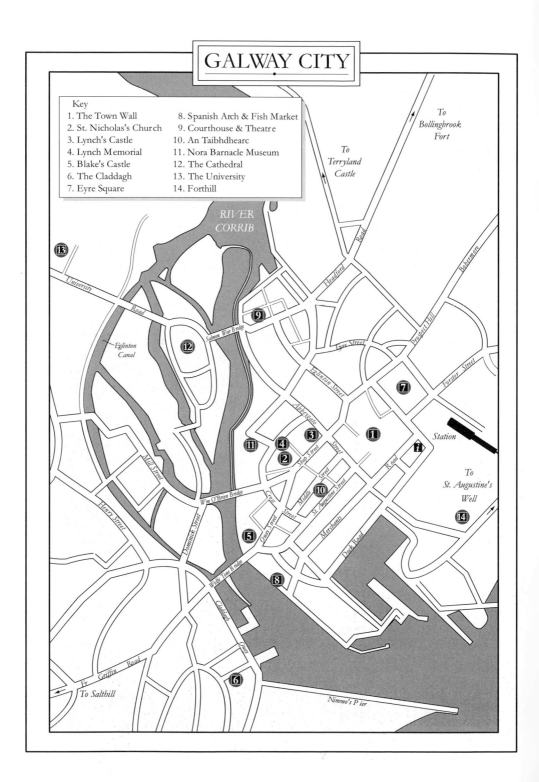

GALWAY CITY

Key
1. The Town Wall
2. St. Nicholas's Church
3. Lynch's Castle
4. Lynch Memorial
5. Blake's Castle
6. The Claddagh
7. Eyre Square
8. Spanish Arch & Fish Market
9. Courthouse & Theatre
10. An Taibhdhearc
11. Nora Barnacle Museum
12. The Cathedral
13. The University
14. Forthill

RIVER CORRIB

To Bollingbrook Fort

To Terryland Castle

Bohermore

University Road

Headford Road

Eyre Street

Prospect Hill

Forster Street

Eglinton Canal

Salmon Weir Bridge

Eglinton Street

Station

Mill Street

Abbeygate

Shop Street

To St. Augustine's Well

Henry Street

Wm O'Brien Bridge

Cross Street

Middle Street

St. Augustine Street

Merchants Road

Dock Road

Dominick Street

Wolfe Tone Bridge

Quay Street

Claddagh Quay

Fr Griffin Road

To Salthill

Nimmo's Pier

THE RIVER CORRIB

The River Corrib or, to give its legal title, the River of Galway is a short but very significant river because it is the means whereby the surplus waters of the great expanses of Loughs Corrib, Mask and Carra are carried to the sea. From where it exits Lough Corrib to the regulating weir at Woodquay, a distance of some five kilometres, the river flows in a gentle serpentine of smooth, clear water. It then divides into a number of branches with the main channel on the east carrying the bulk of the waters below the weir. Alongside and to the west a venous system of smaller rivers surround the natural contours of a series of islands before rejoining the parent channel again as they enter the sea at O'Brien Bridge.

In recent years numerous objects have been recovered from the riverbed above the weir, ranging in date from prehistoric stone axes, swords and spearheads to nineteenth-century bottles and clay pipes – all testifying to the extensive traffic on its waters since earliest times. The Vikings used the river in AD927 on their way to plunder island settlements on Lough Corrib, and in the late medieval period it was crossed frequently by marauding parties in search of plunder and spoils.

Where the River Corrib flows: Galway and its waterways.

The river was anciently called the Gaillimh and from it the Anglo-Norman settlement took its name, gradually anglicised as Galway. It was only in the eighteenth century that the name River Corrib began to replace the older form. The origin of the name Gaillimh is uncertain and has been the subject of some debate among toponymists and onomastic experts. Legend – that least reliable of sources – records that it was named after a woman called Gailleamh who drowned here. She was the daughter of king Breasal, who is associated with the mythological island Hy Brazil. Folklore and literary invention apart, the explanation generally accepted is that Gaillimh is related to the word *gall*, an old Irish word for stone. However, being a river name, its roots may go back beyond recorded history.

The river has always been an integral part of the lives of Galway people and over the centuries has provided them with sustenance (through its extensive salmon and eel fisheries), power (for their mills), transport (for goods coming to and from the markets) and recreation (through the numerous boating and angling clubs). One of the great sights in Galway was the summer salmon run when the shoals gathered just above the Salmon Weir Bridge. The black sheen along the edge of the parapet testifies to the countless people who have stood here, gazing down at the multitudes of dark shadows below, which quietly rest here before making the final leap to their destined spawning grounds.

The system of waterways that greets the visitor today is largely the result of the major drainage and navigation schemes carried out in the mid-nineteenth century. The works included the construction of the Eglinton Canal and tidal basin and a total refurbishment of all the old mill-races. With the demise of the canal and mills in the twentieth century, many of the smaller water-courses were neglected and became choked with weeds and rubbish. But thanks to the Galway Civic Trust and the corporation they have now taken on a new life and are being developed as a civic amenity. A leisurely stroll along the canal and new riverside path, Bruach na Coiribe (the bank of the Corrib) between Wolfe Tone Bridge and Newtownsmith will enhance your awareness of the importance of these waterways in the city's history. Once they provided power to industry, now they are preserves for a whole range of wetland flora and fauna. And if the river is in spate, you will encounter at first-hand the raw power of nature. By way of counterbalance, take a boat-trip on the river above Woodquay and be rewarded with an appreciation of the diversity and richness of its calmer waters and scenery – an experience shared by countless others who have journeyed this way over the millennia.

THE TOWN WALLS

The earliest account of the walling of Galway dates to around 1270 and, though we do not know for certain when it was completed, significant stretches were in existence in the fourteenth century. Most, if not all of the town was enclosed by the early fifteenth century. The total area within the walls, amounting to about eleven hectares (c.twenty-seven acres), was quite small in comparison with some of the other major medieval ports, such as Dublin, Waterford and Limerick, which were twice its size; Drogheda and New Ross were even larger still.

The remains of the town wall at the rear of Spanish Arch.

There were four gate-houses or entrances into the town and the walls were strengthened by the addition of at least seven substantial towers positioned at strategic points. The main thoroughfare from the east, An Bóthar Mór (the Great Road), now anglicised as Bohermore, led to the principal entrance, the Great Gate, which was situated in the middle of the eastern curtain wall. This stood at the east end of present William Street and was further protected by an outwork or barbican – a rectangular walled and defended courtyard. The second entrance, the Little Gate, stood at the end of Abbeygate

Street Upper, near the junction with Mary Street, and led to the Franciscan friary and northern suburbs on St Stephen's Island. The third gate was situated at the West Bridge (on the site of present O'Brien Bridge) and the fourth opened onto the quays at the end of Quay Street, hence its name (see Phillips's prospect of the quay area, p.106). There were also a number of other smaller gates or passages opening onto the sea and river and used by boatmen and fishermen.

Aware of the vulnerability of their eastern defences, especially after the widespread use of cannon, the townspeople added massive stone bastions on this side between 1646 and 1651. A small section of one of these still survives at the rear of Dunnes Stores, Eyre Square, and the outline and string-course of another, which flanked the old barbican in front of the Great Gate, can be seen in the obtuse angle of the buildings at the northern end of Ballalley Lane. The foundations of a huge, diamond-shaped bastion defending the southern corner were uncovered in the late 1980s in the course of pre-development excavations on the site of the Eyre Square Centre. A plaque from this work, dated 1647 and carved with the Galway coat of arms, is preserved in the City Museum at the Spanish Arch. Three other similar plaques survive from this period and can be seen on the corner of the Lion's Tower building (Eglinton Street), and on the

Foundations of the diamond-shaped bastion (built 1647) uncovered during excavations in 1989, now beneath the Eyre Square Centre.

façades of the Imperial Hotel (Eyre Square) and the appropriately named Galway Arms Inn (Dominick Street).

The surviving stretches of the walls are not particularly imposing, but if you stand at the quayside behind Spanish Arch you can form a tolerably convincing impression of what they must have looked like around the remainder of the town. However, you must allow for the fact that the sea originally came up to the wall at this point and you are standing about one-and-a-half metres above the original shoreline. A portion of the parapet wall here is carried on corbels (projecting stone brackets) and the spaces between the brackets (now blocked up) were once open to allow missiles to be dropped on would-be assailants. Likewise, a visit to the Eyre Square Centre will reward the viewer with prospects from different levels of what is probably the oldest section of the wall. The lower courses of the two wall-towers uncovered there – the New Tower/Shoemakers' Tower and the Pipar's/Pipe/Penrice's Tower (depending on which map you choose to follow) – were built up to the height of the adjoining town wall.

ARMS OF THE CITY

Since its foundation in the early thirteenth century the town of Galway has used five different coats of arms. The first three of these did not, as far as is known, belong to the town proper but were used by townspeople for official purposes in the absence of a specific town arms. The earliest set, comprising a red cross on a gold shield, date from about 1270 onwards and were those of the de Burgo family, earls of Ulster. In 1368 the de Burgo possessions passed, by marriage, into the control of Edmund Mortimer, earl of March (in England), and Galway began to use his arms, now combined with those of his wife, through whom the earldom had come into his possession. In heraldry the usual manner of representing an alliance of two great families is by dividing the shield into four parts and placing the respective arms in the opposing quarters. In this instance, the upper-left and bottom-right quarters contain the original de Burgo arms and the two other quarters show the Mortimer arms (a series of horizontal bars of gold and blue with a superimposed plain silver shield).

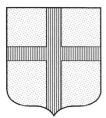

The de Burgo arms.

Galway's fifteenth-century arms.

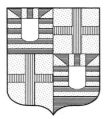

Arms of the earls of Mortimer.

The Galway arms as we know them today, on the plaque, dated 1646, from the former Lion Tower Bastion, Eglinton Street.

A variation on the current arms used in the eighteenth and nine-teenth centuries.

The next set of Galway arms began to be used by the town officials in the fifteenth century and consist of a blue shield on which appears a golden chevron and three silver castles. Little is known about them and they appear to be derived from personal arms. Indeed, they bear a remarkable resemblance to the arms of a prominent Galway family, the Lynchs. Both have the same shield colour and gold chevron: the only difference is that the Lynch arms have three trefoils instead of castles. This new set did not supersede the Ulster–March arms, and both were in simultaneous use. The reason why they came to be used is probably related to the fact that this was a period of growing independence for the town and the adoption by some townspeople of a different set of arms – one that did not hint at allegiance to any former lord or master – was one further public declaration of their intentions.

Galway finally managed to get its independence in 1484 and it was only natural that its citizens should ultimately want a new coat of arms to mark them out as different and special. However, we do not know precisely when this was decided upon. All we can say is that sometime after 1578 – possibly when the charter was renewed in 1580 – a new set of arms were granted to the town. These, the fourth set, are the arms as we know them today. They consist of a golden, single-masted galley with sails furled, floating on waves and placed on a silver shield. Hanging from the mast is a smaller, black shield bearing the device of a golden lion. The galley clearly represents the town's maritime trading connections, but the origin of the golden lion is unclear. The central design (the galley with a hanging shield) has remained constant, though in a number of instances the shield is shown not with the golden lion but with a version of the royal arms of England, that is, a quartering of the arms of France and England formerly used by English sovereigns. This variant (the fifth official set) was used occasionally by the corporation in the late eighteenth and early nineteenth centuries. Why this was so is a mystery, and no satisfactory explanation for its occurrence has been found.

THE TRIBES OF GALWAY

Galway has long been known as the City of the Tribes, and its history is associated with the fortunes of a particular group of families who have come to be known as the Tribes of Galway. The precise origin of this name is unknown and would appear to have been adopted by the old Catholic ruling families after the Cromwellian capture of the town in

Arms of the fourteen 'Tribes of Galway'.

1652 as a mark of honour, a means of distinguishing themselves from the new arrivals. Although it has been suggested that it may have originated as a term of reproach by the Cromwellian soldiers, the earliest reference to the use of the name is encountered on the famous Pictorial Map of mid-seventeenth-century Galway, printed during the reign of Charles II (1660–1685) (*see* p.34). On this map fourteen families are singled out and described rather proudly as 'tribes' and compared grandly with the seven tribes of ancient Rome. Indeed, the metaphor is carried to extreme in the verses which accompany the coats of arms blazoned along the bottom of the map where it is boasted that Galway is the Rome of Connacht! The fourteen families identified are: Athy, Blake, Bodkin, Browne, Darcy, Deane, Font, French, Joyce, Kirwan, Lynch, Martin, Morris and Skerrett.

Why, how or who agreed to this selection is unknown. Most of these families could claim, by ancestry and prescription arising from ancient custom, to trace their roots back in time to the founding of the town. Certainly, many were Anglo-Norman in origin and followers of the de Burgos who, in the wake of the invasion of Connacht in the early thirteenth century, gradually came and settled in the town. Others, such as the Kirwans and Darcys, were of Gaelic origin. Over the years they managed to integrate themselves into the social fabric of the town and become an integral part of the local patriciate. It was largely through the efforts of Blake, Browne, Darcy, French, Kirwan, Lynch and Martin families that Galway developed into one of the most important port towns in Ireland. And with their background, wealth and education they rose to positions of power in both the local administration and the Church.

Undoubtedly, the most successful of the 'tribes' were the Lynchs, who were certainly established in Galway by the late thirteenth century. The family possesses an extraordinary record at local government level. The first mayor of the town was a Lynch, and between 1485 and 1654 – the year when the last mayor elected by the old Galway families was deposed by the Cromwellian governor – over eighty members of that family had held this office.

It was not always certain how many families constituted the 'tribes'. In the eighteenth century some lists excluded either the Deane, Font or Morris families, obviously believing that their members did not play a particularly important role in the civic history of the town. The publication, in 1820, of the *History of Galway* by James Hardiman settled once and for all the exact number of 'tribes' as fourteen, but the establishment of the Catholic diocese of Galway in 1831 effectively extinguished their quasi-official power in local Church politics. It is important to remember that this specific group of families was never given formal recognition in any grant or charter and the so-called 'tribes of Galway' did not possess legal authority or validity. The names of many of the 'tribes' are still to be found around the city and its environs, though a number – Athy, Deane, Font and Skerrett – are largely extinct.

SWORD AND MACE

The privilege of carrying a sword and/or mace was granted by monarchs in the Middle Ages to mayors of certain towns and cities. The Galway civic sword dates to 1610 when James I established the town as a separate county, distinct from the county at large. As a mark of this new honour the mayor was extended the right to have a sword borne before him on ceremonial occasions. It is not known when Galway first was granted the right to bear a mace. The earliest mention of one dates from the visit of lord deputy Sir Thomas Ratcliffe to the town in 1558. This was probably a small mace, but neither it nor its successors (if there were any) have survived. The present great mace was presented to the town in 1712 by its mayor, Edward Eyre.

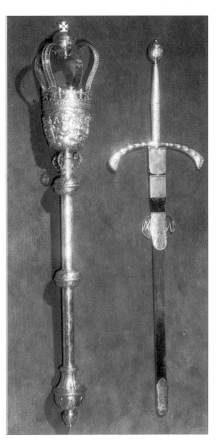

The Galway civic sword (1610) and mace (1712).

On the abolition of the corporation in 1841 both the sword and mace were given to the last mayor, Edmond Blake, as some form of compensation for his loss of office. They ultimately came into the possession of the American newspaper tycoon William Randolph Hearst, whose career inspired the Orson Welles's film *Citizen Kane* (1941). Shortly before his death in 1951, Hearst expressed the wish that they should be returned to Galway to the municipal corporation, which had been restored to the city in 1937, and in 1960 the Hearst Foundation generously presented them to the town. The sword and mace are now on display in the Bank of Ireland premises, 19 Eyre Square, and are still borne before the mayor and corporation on ceremonial occasions.

The Galway civic sword is very much a real weapon. Its double-edged, steel blade is of German origin and belonged to a type of sword in use in the sixteenth century and known as a Two-Hander. These were substantial weapons and in the appropriate hands were used to devastating effect in battle. Both the hilt and scabbard date from the period when the weapon was converted into use as a civic sword (shortly after 1610) and the metal used throughout in these parts is silver. The four silver mounts on the scabbard tell us much about the weapon's history.

The two oldest fittings are the chape (at the bottom of the scabbard, covering the sword point) and the locket or mount at the mouth, which appear to be contemporary with the making of the civic sword. On the front of the locket is a spirited engraving of the Galway coat of arms with the galley shown flying an English flag, while the back of the locket contains a secondary inscription recording the restoration of the monarchy in England in 1660. The chape also bears a secondary inscription but it was deliberately obliterated some time after its completion. The little that can be made out refers to the notorious Colonel Peter Stubbers, the Cromwellian soldier who was appointed military governor of Galway shortly after its surrender in 1652. It was he who ousted the mayor, Thomas Lynch fitz Ambrose, from office in 1654 and had himself elected in his place. Stubbers was hated by the townspeople and it seems likely that when the sword came back into the hands of the Catholics during James II's, time his inscription was erased.

The next oldest fitting is the inscribed, ornamental mount bearing the royal cipher WM (for William and Mary) in the open-worked wings on either side. This was added to the scabbard in 1692 or shortly after. In the eighteenth century various mayors flattered their vanity by having their names inscribed on the back of this piece and on the chape: Charles Revett Senior (1727), Corasdaile Shaw (1746 and 1759), John Shaw (1755), Patrick Blake (1756), Charles Revett Junior (1761) and Patrick Blake of Drum (1771). The final addition to the scabbard, just below the mouth-piece, was put there in 1876 or soon after when the sword was in the possession of Edmond Blake, the last mayor of Galway. The inscription relates to his father, Colonel John Blake (mayor, 1830), and to himself (mayor and deputy mayor, 1831–1841).

The mace is made of silver and is of a form that had become standard by the end of the seventeenth century. It consists of a massive staff topped with a bowl surmounted by a full crown, complete with fillet, cresting, arches, orb and cross. It was made in Dublin between 1708 and 1710 and is richly decorated in the Baroque style. The shaft is ornamented throughout with incised patterns of roses and thistles growing from the same twinning stem. The surface of the bowl is divided by four caryatids (nude female demi-figures) into compartments that are filled with various devices or badges representing England, Scotland, France and Ireland, each set between the letters AR – *Anna Regina* – the monogram of Queen Anne. The orb on top of the crown that surmounts the bowl is inscribed: *Ex dono Edwardi Eyre major de Gallway An° Dom^e 1712* – the gift of Edward Eyre, mayor of Galway, in the year of the Lord 1712. The terminal to the shaft is in the form of an acorn and the upper surface of the knob above it is divided into four panels, each of which is ornamented with similar devices to those on the bowl to represent the various countries. The lower section includes engravings of both the arms of Galway and those of Edward Eyre, the donor.

GALWAY STREET NAMES: SIGNPOSTS TO THE PAST

The central core of the city – the area of the old walled town – is a web of narrow streets and lanes, each with its own distinctive name and every one with its own story to tell. They are small time capsules, signposts directing us to places or activities that are long forgotten, reminding us of trades, families and individuals who had some special

connection with the city down through the centuries. Some names are very old and date to the early beginnings of the town; some are quite new. Their survival, however, has been fortuitous.

The rich and varied nature of the city's street names is reflected in those of the principal east–west thoroughfare from Eyre Square to O'Brien Bridge, which, though only 350 metres in length, is known by five different names. The eastern section, from Lynch's Castle to Eyre Square, is divided into William Street and Williamsgate Street respectively, both dating from the close of the seventeenth century and commemorating the English king William III, the victor at the Battle of the Boyne in 1690. This street was previously known as Great Gate Street after the principal town gate, which stood at its eastern end. The section from Lynch's Castle as far as the junction with High Street is called Shop Street. This is not a very old name and only came into being in the eighteenth century when the first shops were opened here. It was formerly known as High Middle Street, 'high' being a synonym for 'main' or 'principal'. From here to the next junction (i.e., with Cross Street) it is named Mainguard Street. The old Tholsel (corresponding to the present civic offices of the corporation), which included the town jail, stood at the western end of this street. It also accommodated a military guard and, as a consequence, became known as the Mainguard, hence the present name. The final section of this thoroughfare is Bridge Street. In the seventeenth century the name possessed the additional element 'gate' and was known as Bridge-gate Street, in effect confirming the former presence of a gate at this end of the bridge. Until the nineteenth century this was the only link between the town and its western suburbs. It was renamed William O'Brien Bridge in 1889 after the Irish author and nationalist MP (d.1928) who was then serving a prison sentence in the county jail on Nuns' Island. This latter name dates from the mid-seventeenth century when the Poor Clare nuns (who have been in residence there since 1825) were granted permission to erect a convent here.

Street names like Kirwan's Lane, Eyre Square and Newtownsmith are called after particular families (or in the case of the last, one indi-vidual – Erasmus Smith) who had extensive property holdings in these areas. The explanation for other names, for example, Quay Street, Cross Street and Middle Street, likewise is almost self-explanatory in that they incorporate elements descriptive of their location or function. Quay Street led to the old medieval quays, which were in front of present-day Spanish Arch – a name that is com-pletely modern. Cross Street is simply the street which crossed the main east–west thoroughfare and Middle Street is, as its name suggests, situated mid-way between present-day Shop Street and St Augustine Street.

St Augustine Street officially came into being on 25 September 1858 when the town commissioners unanimously decided to change it in honour of the Augustinian friars who had built a new church there. The street was formerly known as Back Street because it was at the back or more remote end of the town: the town wall ran through the middle of the present buildings on its southern side. In earlier times it was known as New Tower Street (i.e., the street that led to the New Tower at the southeast corner of the town walls, which can be seen in the Eyre Square Centre). The western extension of this street is called Flood Street for the simple reason that it was subject to flooding, especially at the spring high tides. Merchants' Road was built in 1779 and was initially called New Cross Street, but its present form became the accepted norm on account of the many merchants who had erected warehouses and stores along it.

Perhaps the oldest of the surviving names is Lombard Street, so-called after the Lombards of Italy whose merchants and bankers con-trolled much of the trade in wool and hides in Ireland in the late thir-teenth and early fourteenth centuries. Galway had a considerable export in both items at this period, and it seems likely that the Lom-bards or their agents carried on business somewhere in this street. One might be forgiven for thinking that Abbeygate Street is also a very old name, but in fact it only dates from the first half of the eight-eenth century. It replaced the earlier form, Littlegate Street (i.e., the street leading to the Little Gate as opposed to the Great Gate), which led to the Franciscan friary outside the town. Since its foundation in 1296 this friary has been known as the Abbey, the name that is still used today by most Galwegians. Among the newer streets is Eglinton Street. It was laid out in 1851 along the line of the old town wall and named after the lord lieutenant, the duke of Eglinton, who visited Galway in the following year to open the newly constructed canal that also bears his name.

The narrow section of the street known as Bowling Green serves to remind us of the former popularity of this particular sport; in the eighteenth century there was a small bowling green situated on its north side. Another sporting connection is indicated by the name Ballalley Lane (off Williamsgate Street) and refers to the fact that ball games were once played here against the old town wall. Buttermilk Lane, between Shop Street and St Augustine Street, tells its own story of local trade. In much earlier times it was the scene of a different craft for it was known as Shoemakers' Lane. Indeed, we know that there was a considerable leather-working industry in the town because another street, present Abbeygate Street Lower, was known in the earlier seventeenth century as Skinners' or Glovers' Street.

But everything is not what it might seem at first for some names have moved with the times. The explanation for present-day Market Street originates with the corn and butter markets that were held here. The former was moved to the east of the town in 1810, and the latter, now considerably expanded, has taken up permanent residence outside the railings of St Nicholas's Church ever since an open space was created there in the early 1820s (strictly speaking, most of this market is held in Lombard Street). In the mid-seventeenth century Market Street was called North Street, and present-day High Street was called Market Street.

Some streets also have undergone quite a few name changes over the centuries. For example, the small lane connecting Quay Street with Flood Street first appears in history as Bóthar an Iarla – the Earl's Lane – named after Richard de Burgo, the Red Earl (d.1326); the foundations of his castle and hall were revealed recently following archaeological excavations at the rear of the Custom House. It became known as Court House Lane in the late seventeenth century following the building of a county courthouse at its southern end in

1686. As this was used for a short period between the assizes as a
Mass house by the Augustinian friars it may explain the name Chapel
Lane, which is carved on the stone plaque at its northern end. In the
early nineteenth century it was known as Holland's Lane, presumably
after a family of that name who lived there. And in 1996 Galway corporation officially changed the name to Druid Lane to celebrate the
twenty-first anniversary of the internationally renowned Druid
Theatre Company whose theatre is situated here.

GALWAY, A HERITAGE IN STONE

Galway is renowned for its rich architectural inheritance, a product
of its golden age, c.1450–1650, when numerous fine houses and
mansions were built. Visitors at that time remarked on the elegance
of their 'fair and stately buildings ... all of hewed stone, garnished
with fair battlements, in a uniform course, as if the whole town had
been built upon one model.' The stone in question is the local, grey-
blue limestone, which lends itself to the sculpting of exquisite detail.
Some of the finest carvings are to be found on St Nicholas's Church
and Lynch's Castle, though good collections have been gathered
together for display in Lynch's Café, Shop Street, and in the City
Museum at the Spanish Arch. There is much to reward the diligent
searcher for many examples can be seen by looking carefully at the
upper parts of the façades where they peep out from the rendering
amid the shop signs. The majority originally formed parts of windows,

Doorway, dated 1577, from the Athy House, St Augustine Street
(photo 1938), now in storage at the Galway City Museum.

doorways or fireplaces salvaged from old ruins in the city, and have been preserved as much for their decorative and curiosity value as out of any sense of their intrinsic worth.

Although Galway once had extensive commercial contacts with Spain, there is little to suggest that its buildings are of Spanish style or origin – a fancy popularised by ill-informed travel writers in the nineteenth century. The surviving architectural remains are best described as a mixture of two styles: firstly, the English Tudor style (largely Gothic in detail but owing its *raison d'être* to the Renaissance movement) and secondly, the Elizabethan and Jacobean style (classic in detail but somewhat inaccurate in application and proportion). The essential Gothic elements – the pointed arch, mouldings and other ornamental details – are found in profusion throughout the town, especially its dominant motif: the vine leaf. But all these details were rendered in a distinctively Irish manner. For example, Gaelic influences can be seen in the incorporation of interlace work in the carving. Fine examples are found on Lynch's Castle, the Athy doorway (dated 1577 and now in storage at the Spanish Arch) and St Nicholas's Church.

The Browne doorway in its original location in Abbeygate Street Lower (c.1900).

It was only in the early seventeenth century that the true classical ideas, which had become commonplace in England, filtered westwards and began to gain a foothold in Galway. There is a stark contrast between this and the earlier work. Gone are the pointed arch and the vine decoration to be replaced by the rounded arch, columns, plinths, entablatures and other ornamental detailing. However, the sophistication of the true classical forms was not fully understood by provincial masons and the surviving architecture from this time displays a certain rudimentary character. But this is its charm. It exhibits a snapshot of the values and aspirations of the wealthy merchants who wanted the very latest in Jacobean style and fashion. Pre-eminent among the surviving examples are the Browne and Darcy doorways. The former (dated 1627) stands at the top of Eyre Square and the latter (dated 1624) has been re-erected in the private grounds of the Convent of Mercy, Francis Street.

For the student of heraldry the numerous coats of arms around the city are of special interest. The earliest surviving examples date to the late fifteenth century and are to be seen on Lynch's Castle. By the middle of the sixteenth century we see a gradual increase in the use and display of such arms, and they became especially popular as decorative emblems on fireplace lintels in the early seventeenth century. The arms are often accompanied by a date and the initials of the husband and wife. Though generally referred to as marriage stones, there is no evidence to support the oft-repeated suggestion that the date indicates the year of marriage. More than likely the date refers to the year in which the piece was made.

Alongside some coats of arms and usually surrounded by a shield – thereby giving them a certain armigerous character – will be found a series of other symbols known as merchants' or guilds' marks: the personal sign or mark of individual merchants and traders. We tend to forget that few could read or write at this period and such marks were in everyday use in the town and would have been chalked, painted, branded or carved onto a whole range of materials, goods and commodities. All of these pieces tell us of another world, of other attitudes, of other beliefs and fashions and are a silent witness to the industry and pride of those who lived and worked in old Galway.

The Lynch arms and two merchants' or guilds' marks, Shop Street.

ST NICHOLAS'S CHURCH

Given Galway's long maritime associations, it should come as little surprise to find that its parish church was named after the patron saint of seafarers, St Nicholas of Myra. The church also has connections with one of the world's most famous seafarers as it seems likely that the intrepid explorer Christopher Columbus may have heard Mass here sometime around 1477 when he stopped off at Galway during one of his voyages.

St Nicholas's Church prior to the restoration of the tower parapets in 1883.

St Nicholas's Church is one of the finest medieval parish churches in Ireland and the only medieval ecclesiastical building to survive in Galway. It is essentially a cruciform structure with a long nave, slightly narrower than the chancel, and flanked by exceptionally wide aisles. This gives it a unique triple-gabled façade at its western end. As with many buildings that have been in existence and continuous use for almost 700 years, it has undergone numerous modifications and alterations. Most of the fabric of the building dates from the fourteenth to the sixteenth centuries and subsequent work has been restricted for the most part to internal reorganisation and restoration carried out in the nineteenth and twentieth centuries.

The actual foundation date of St Nicholas's Church must remain conjectural. Although it is generally considered to have been built in 1320, this date appears to relate only to the first major building operation on the site. History tells us that there was a church here in the opening years of the fourteenth century and we can be sure that its foundation goes back well before this time. It began as a dependency of the Cistercian monastery of Knockmoy, some twenty-seven kilometres northeast of the town, was created into a separate vicarage in the 1380s and made collegiate (i.e., comprising a college of eight vicars governed by a warden) in 1484. It was re-established as the Reformed Royal College of Galway in 1551. Recovered by the Catholics between 1643 and 1652 and again for a brief period during the Williamite wars (1689–1691), the church has since been in the hands of Protestant clergy and is now a Church of Ireland (Anglican) parish church. The office of warden was abolished in 1841; the last warden, Rev James Daly, was allowed to remain on until his death in 1865 and the pulpit at the entrance to the chancel was erected in his honour.

The major construction work that took place about 1320 resulted in a substantial cruciform parish church. Fragments of an earlier church can be seen in the exterior of the south wall of the chancel. The tower was added probably towards the end of the fifteenth century and the south aisle followed shortly after in the early years of the sixteenth century. It was begun by a very wealthy merchant, Dominick Duff Lynch, and following his death in 1508 was completed by his son, Stephen, whose coat of arms, together with those of his wife (Margaret Athy), may be seen, along with a merchant's or guild's

mark, flanking the corbel at the junction of the aisle and adjoining transept. The eastern section of the north aisle was widened in 1538 and the remainder completed in 1583: the date is carved on the outside of the gable window. The south porch appears to be a complete refurbishment of a fifteenth-century original, and the south transept was lengthened in 1561 by Dominick's grandson, Nicholas Lynch. The present spire dates from 1683 and the tower parapets were restored in 1883.

The mermaid on the window (dated 1583) of the north aisle.

The most salient features of the exterior are the now-functionless water-spouts, especially the gargoyles, some of them with fantastic creatures and heads. The church also possesses a rich array of window forms that date from the fourteenth to the late sixteenth century, many carved with intricate human, animal and floral detailing, including two mermaids (one on the gable window in the south transept and the other on that of the north aisle).

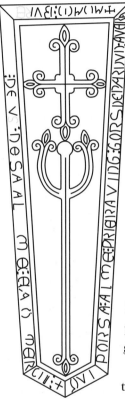

The graveslab of Adam Bure, an Anglo-Norman settler, dated to the late thirteenth/early fourteenth century.

The interior is particularly rich in tombs and other fittings. The baptismal font in the south aisle dates from the late sixteenth/early seventeenth century and is decorated with window forms that echo in miniature those in the north aisle. Of particular interest are the numerous graveslabs and other funerary memorials. The earliest, the grave of one of the Anglo-Norman settlers, dates to the late thirteenth or early fourteenth century and is on the floor of the small chapel, on the right-hand side of the chancel. The inscription in Norman French reads in translation: 'Here lies Adam Bure. May God have mercy on his soul. Whoever will pray for his soul will have twenty days indulgence.'

The next oldest memorials date to the sixteenth century. Principal among these are the two fine graveslabs with interlaced ornament, dated 1577 and 1580, set in the walls of the south transept. This transept also contains three magnificent tombs. In the corner is a very fine chest-tomb with faint traces of red paint still visible in some of the niches. These niches are carved with various coats of arms and a pair of merchants' marks, which are repeated on a plaque set in the gable wall above. This plaque is blank though at one time it undoubtedly had a commemorative painted picture or inscription. Some claim that this is the tomb of the James Lynch Fitz Stephen – the mayor who is reputed to have hung his son –

but this is a complete nonsense. Beside this is a magnificent altar-tomb with a canopy of finely executed flowing tracery. It is enlivened with a representation of the crowned figure of Christ displaying the five wounds. The feet have been smashed – undoubtedly by the Cromwellian soldiery. We do not know for whom the monument was built but it most probably was for a member of the Lynch family, after whom this transept was named. And next to this is another altar flanked by the coats of arms of the Lynch family with angels as candleholders, also, sadly, smashed. The small inset tablet, dated 1644, is a secondary addition.

A remarkable collection of memorials has been assembled as paving slabs in the north aisle and a number of these include occupational symbols of the deceased's trade or guild. One bears a shears with a gloved hand holding a dog(?) on a leash – perhaps a shepherd or leather-worker – another has the trowel and square of a mason, and a third bears three hammers surmounted by crowns, reputedly emblems of a goldsmith. Also in this aisle is the free-standing *Beniter*

or holy-water stoup decorated with vine leaves, probably dating to the fifteenth century. Directly above is the misnamed Lepers' Gallery. This short gallery merely provides access to the bell-tower and has never functioned as anything else; lepers would never have been allowed within the walls of the town, let alone enter the church.

St Nicholas's also contains a miscellany of other memorabilia, including two battle standards and memorials relating to the Connaught Rangers (a division of the British Army, formed in 1793 and disbanded in 1922). Entrance to the Blessed Sacrament Chapel (off the north aisle) is by a reader's

The corbel at the junction of the north aisle and transept showing Joshua returning home from Canaan with the grapes.

desk. This was removed from the old college and erected here in the early nineteenth century. Reader's desks are a common feature of many abbeys and friaries around Ireland and were used during meal-times when a member of the community – in this case, the college – would read extracts from the scriptures. The north transept is now enclosed and contains the Henry Library, transferred here from St Mary's Cathedral, Tuam, in 1985. It formerly belonged to the Rev. Joseph Henry DD (c.1820–1885), a noted bibliophile.

But it is the carved details that fascinate and entertain us most – the gargoyles on the south aisle, the mermaids, animals and other fantastic creatures on the window stops, the hound and hare forever poised on either side above the door leading to the bell-tower, the corbels enlivened with the smiling angel and the belted man (Joshua returning from Canaan with the grapes), the little manticora (lion's body with a man's head) and leaves positioned at the tapering ends of the corbels on the crossing piers – all these little felicities were captured in the mason's fantasy and carved with an intimacy and emotion that still touches us today.

LYNCH'S CASTLE

Situated at the junction of Shop Street and Abbeygate Street Upper, at almost the exact centre of the old medieval town, this castle gives us a glimpse of the architectural elegance that was typical of Galway in the late Middle Ages. It is the finest surviving example of an urban tower-house in the country and is the oldest building in Ireland that is used daily for commercial purposes. Unfortunately, very little is known about the history of the castle and it is not recorded by or for whom it was erected. It was certainly the home of a very wealthy member of the Lynch family and was reputedly the residence of Thomas Lynch fitz Ambrose, mayor of Galway in 1654.

The building has been much modified and altered over the course of its 500-year existence. The oldest portion, at the street junction, consists of a classic tower-house type castle and dates to around 1500. At this time it possessed a smaller western wing, which was subsequently raised, possibly in the seventeenth century, to the height of the adjoining tower and new windows inserted in it. The straight joint between the two structures is clearly visible in the upper part of the Shop Street façade and the difference in the carving of the hood-moulds over the two windows further highlights this later work. There is a record of massive alterations undertaken to the whole structure in the early years of the nineteenth century; since 1918 it has been a bank premises.

The castle was certainly much higher than the surviving remains indicate and it appears originally to have had five storeys, one more than at present. At some stage, most likely in the early nineteenth century, the floor levels were changed and the present orderly arrangement of late Georgian windows inserted. At this time also the older carvings and hood-moulds were moved to their present positions and others may have been added. Some indication of the original floor levels can be gained from the three surviving gun-loops on the corner of the building and from the few remaining examples of windows which are still *in situ*. Between the third and fourth storeys on the Shop Street façade are the blocked-up remains of a large, finely decorated window with cusped ogee heads to the lights: its lower section has been removed. The

Lynch's Castle.

location of such a large window at this level is typical of tower-houses of the period for the principal living-room, or hall as it was called, usually was on the uppermost floor. The remains of two other blocked-up windows can be seen in the masonry of the storey below and it seems likely that the hood-moulds above the present third-storey windows may have been taken from them. On the same level as the blocked-up windows is another single-light example on the Abbeygate Street façade.

Among the carvings deserving particular attention are the merchants' marks – based on a reversed 4 figure – carved below the hood-mould terminals. This particular mark undoubtedly belonged to the original owner, but we do not know his identity. A most unusual feature of the castle is the occurrence of carved water-spouts (eighteen in all), which are now functionless though originally would have carried rainwater from the roof clear of the building. Nine of these are true gargoyles (grotesque animal and human heads) and may be compared with the only other surviving examples from Galway, on St Nicholas's Church.

Merchant's mark.

There are three panels with coats of arms on the castle. The upper circular panel on the Shop Street façade has a shield bearing the Lynch arms accompanied by the simple Latin inscription: *Scutum de Lynche* – Lynch's shield or coat of arms. Immediately below it is the carving of a lion-like creature with the facial characteristics of a human. There is an almost identical figure on the Abbeygate Street façade below another roundel bearing the arms of the FitzGeralds. Directly under each is a stone with a Latin inscription in Gothic letters. That on the Shop Street façade reads: 'After darkness I hope for light', while the other reads: 'He hath put down the mighty from their seat and hath exalted the lowly' (Magnificat; Luke i, 52).

The large rectangular panel at first-floor level in the Shop Street façade bears the royal arms of Henry VII (1485–1509) accompanied by a contracted Latin inscription in Gothic letters: 'Long live the King of England, France and Lord of Ireland'. The likely explanation for the occurrence of the royal arms on the castle is that the citizens/owners wished to express their loyalty to the new king in light of the 1484 ruling that allowed the town to elect its own mayor and bailiffs with all the special privileges that this entailed. Immediately below this panel is a most unusual carving. It has been generally interpreted as representing an ape holding a child in its paws, but the creature is actually much more lion-like in appearance. The carving is said to represent the story of how a pet monkey or ape rescued a child from a fire in the castle, but this is purely the stuff of myth and legend. A similar story is associated with the FitzGerald family, earls of Kildare, although there may be some truth to it in this instance for a chained ape is the device used as a crest in their coat of arms, which can be seen in the roundel on the Abbeygate Street façade where the FitzGerald arms are carved. The occurrence of these arms on the castle is puzzling, but together with the two inscriptions noted above it might be considered as an expression of gratitude to Garret, earl of Kildare, who came to the assistance of the burgesses in 1504 after William Burke and other chieftains had rebelled and taken the town.

Although built within a walled town the castle incorporated a number of defensive elements, including the gun-loops on the corner and a small, box-like projection on the Abbeygate Street façade. Though much rebuilt, this latter feature houses another loop pointing away from the castle to the north, which probably served to protect a door immediately beside it. Above and to left of it are a curious pair of decorated corbels or brackets. Sitting on top of each one is a perforated block, both of which are later additions. It is thought that the corbels indicate where a bell was hung or where a beam supported some form of block-and-tackle arrangement for hoisting goods into the upper storeys of the castle. Indeed, it is very probable that the latter arrangement existed at one time for there are indications that an arched doorway had been broken through the wall at this point, between the corbels. However, it seems likely that the corbels originally supported a machicolation above the main entrance to the castle (a form of walled-in chute from which missiles could be fired or dropped on would-be attackers below). Such a feature may be seen on Blake's Castle in Quay Street.

The foyer of the bank contains a very fine fireplace moved here from an adjoining premises in the 1930s. It is typical of many which graced the great Galway houses in the sixteenth and seventeenth centuries. The lintel is decorated with an incised joggled pattern in imitation of cut stonework and the keystone is carved with the monogram IHS (a contraction of the Greek form of the name Jesus) surmounted by a cross. Below this are the initials of the husband and wife, RB (probably Blake or Browne) and IF (probably French), and above the date: 1629.

THE LYNCH MEMORIAL

The Lynch Memorial is one of Galway's most famous landmarks and tourist attractions. Situated in Market Street, at the edge of the graveyard attached to St Nicholas's Church, it has all the appearance of being the remains of a genuine late medieval house. Nothing could be farther from the truth, however, for this wall is entirely fake and was built originally in 1854 at a cost of £11. Genuine old window and door fragments, a keystone from a fireplace lintel and other bits and pieces were brought together and assembled to look like an old façade. The reason behind this is recounted on the rectangular panel below the large window, which bears the following inscription:

> This ancient memorial of the stern and unbending justice of the chief magistrate of this city, James Lynch Fitzstephen, elected mayor A.D. 1493, who condemned and executed his own guilty son Walter on this spot, has been restored to this its ancient site A.D. 1854 with the approval of the Town Commissioners by their chairman, V. Revd. Peter Daly, P.P. & Vicar of St. Nicholas.

The 'ancient memorial' to which it refers is the small, gable-shaped stone inset in the wall directly below it, which is carved with a skull and cross-bones. The stone is dated 1624 and is inscribed: 'remember deathe vaniti of vaniti & all is but vaniti.' Both the carving and inscription are typical of memorials found in graveyards of this period, the latter based on the well-known epigram from the Old

Testament (Ecclesiastes 12:8). It formerly had been set over the doorway
of a house that stood on this
spot. The plaque – and by
association the house –
became identified in
local folk tradition with
the story of how, in 1493,
the mayor of Galway
hanged his own son from
the window of his house as
an example to posterity
because his son had
broken trust with a
stranger and murdered
him. These are the essen-
tial elements of the tale
and, regrettably, it is not
possible to establish if
there is any truth in it.

Lynch's Memorial, dated 1624.

When James Hardiman came to write his *History of Galway* (published in 1820), he unfortunately allowed historical accuracy to fall
victim to his desire to relate a good yarn and included a completely
romanticised version of the story, which he had adapted from a historical novel, *George the Third* (1807), by the Rev. Edward Mangin.

Hardiman's melodramatic account was soon accepted as the official version and has been developed and embellished over the years.
You are still likely to hear it poignantly recounted in Galway to this
day! However, there is no evidence whatsoever to link either this
plaque or the house in which it stood with the story or anyone mentioned in it. Nonetheless, it was not long until people were convinced
that this was the *very* window at which the dreadful deed had been
carried out! And so the monument entered the literature and local
parlance as the Lynch Window or the Lynch Memorial Window and
was accepted as fact until the whole story was demythologised by the
historian Dr James Mitchell in the late 1960s. By this time, the fabric
of the wall, no less than the tale, had begun to crumble, but such was
its drawing power for tourists that it was decided to re-erect the

façade exactly as it was – stone for stone – preserving it as monument in its own right.

In 1978 the whole memorial was dismantled and reassembled with a concrete backing. It was set a little back from the pavement so that it could be viewed properly. Two side walls were erected to link it to the boundary wall and these were flanked with pillars which formerly were gate piers into the churchyard beside it. Inset into the right-hand pier is a tablet that reads: 'Lynch Memorial Window Re-sited 1978'. This is an unfortunate choice of wording for it has the effect of deflecting attention away from the real 'memorial', that is, the 1624 plaque for which the whole façade was built in the first place.

Finally, one other myth may also be debunked. Many people have considered that the terms Lynch Law and Lynching derive from this story. The reality, however, is more mundane. The term originated either from Colonel Charles Lynch (1736–1796), of Virginia, USA or from Captain William Lynch, also of Virginia, who was indemnified in 1782 for carrying out illegal punishments.

BLAKE'S CASTLE

Blake's Castle stands at the southern end of Quay Street, beside the Fish Market, just inside the line of the now-vanished town wall. Although exaggerated claims have been made about its antiquity, the present building is not older than the fifteenth century. It is a typical late medieval, urban tower-house, one of a number of such buildings that formerly existed in the city. These castles formed the principal type of fortified dwelling of minor notabilities over much of Ireland in the period between 1450 and 1650.

Blake's Castle is a typical example, preserving a number of interesting features, including the unusual corner window with its cusped trefoil heads. The principal room in the castle was generally on the uppermost floor. Here you will find the largest windows, in this case two of them looking out onto the present Fish Market area where the old medieval quays were sited. Of particular interest is the restored machicolation at roof level in the centre of the façade. This was a defensive feature found on many tower-houses, over the main door, and it enabled the occupiers to hurl missiles on would-be assailants below. Although located within a walled town, the builders clearly saw the need for this additional protection for their dwelling. The building was much larger and longer than the surviving section suggests. A substantial northern section was demolished in the later nineteenth century.

A sketch of Blake's Castle, drawn in the late eighteenth century.

The castle has had a somewhat chequered history. In the aftermath of the Cromwellian land confiscation in the mid-seventeenth century it was taken from the Blakes and granted to a family called Morgan who, in 1686, leased it for use as a county jail. It served in this capacity for the following 125 years. However, it does not appear to have been a very secure establishment for during the winter of 1800 eight prisoners escaped by undermining its walls. The castle ceased to be a prison in 1811 when the new county jail opened on Nuns' Island. It subsequently was used as a store and, later still, housed an electricity transformer. The building was given a new lease of life in the 1990s when it was converted into an attractive restaurant, preserving the earlier features.

THE CLADDAGH

The Claddagh, known the length and breadth of the country through its association with the famous Claddagh ring, is the name of a small suburb situated on the west side of the River Corrib where it enters the sea. It takes its name from the Irish word *an cladach,* meaning a flat, stony shore; prior to the building of the canal basin and quay walls in the mid-nineteenth century, this is precisely how the shoreline must have looked from earliest times. Nothing now survives to indicate the former presence here of a thriving fishing village with its haphazardly arranged cobbled streets and open spaces lined with thatched houses.

There was a settlement here in medieval times that was served by a small chapel belonging to the Premonstratensian canons of Tuam. At the close of the fifteenth century it was granted to the Dominicans and ever since that time the friars have been an integral part of the Claddagh's story. Their present church (opened 1891) is worthy of a visit and contains a fine seventeenth-century wooden statue of Our Lady. The pearl rosary beads adorning the statue was the gift of a Claddagh sailor who brought them home from Jerusalem. At the entrance to the Claddagh (near Wolfe Tone Bridge) stands the statue of Fr Tom Burke (1830–1883), a Dominican and native of Galway, who was one of the most famous preachers of his time in Ireland. The statue was sculpted by Seán Kavanagh (Cork) and unveiled in 1948.

Little is known about the nature or extent of the early settlement at the Claddagh, and its evolution from town suburb to separate 'village', with a distinct identity, appears to have been a gradual process, a product of historical circumstance. There is no evidence that the Claddagh was perceived as a distinct Irish town, as existed at Athlone, Kilkenny or Limerick, and those who lived here in late medieval times were probably seen as being similar to the inhabitants of the other suburbs, most of whom were probably of Gaelic Irish origin. Nonetheless, it may be identified as the abode of the 'sea men' who, in 1585, were forbidden to take up either the plough or the spade lest such occupations prevent them from fishing. It was only after the Cromwellian and Williamite wars of the seventeenth century that a clear distinction, based on religion and country of origin, crept into the governing and social frameworks of the town, separating, both physically and legally, those who were distinctly

On the eve of destruction: an aerial photo of the Claddagh taken in 1928.

Irish and Catholic from those who were not. This exclusion meant that those who resided in the Claddagh area were forced to evolve their own structures alongside those in the town. To a certain extent it was a mutually beneficial coexistence. At its most basic level, the town needed food and the villagers needed a market for their fish.

Much of our knowledge of the Claddagh derives from the numerous nineteenth-century travel writers who have given us vivid pen-pictures of the inhabitants and how they differed in language, dress and customs from those who dwelt in the town. By this time the Claddagh truly was a world apart. The head of the community, known as the mayor or king, ruled according to accepted custom and arbitrated on all disputes. It was he who led out the fleet at the beginning of the herring season in mid-August, after the boats were blessed by a Dominican priest. Having landed their catch it was divided in equal shares among the fishermen. Then the women took control and sold it at the market in Galway, leaving the men with sufficient funds to repair their boats and indulge in the essential luxuries of life: whiskey and tobacco.

The Claddagh fishermen sailed a particular type of craft, which, depending on size, was known as the Hooker or *Bád Mór* (the Big Boat, about forty feet long), the Half Boat or *Leath Bhád* (about thirty-two feet long), the *Gleóteog* (between twenty-four and

The Claddagh, Galway

Some of the inhabitants of the Claddagh village in the
late nineteenth/early twentieth century.

twenty-eight feet long), possibly from *gleóite,* meaning pretty, and
the *Púcán* – no real English equivalent (about twenty-four feet long).
Saved from extinction by a handful of enthusiasts, these boats are
now enjoying a revival. In 1820 there were 250 fishing boats operating out of the Claddagh, most of which were *Gleóteogs* or *Púcáns.*
Everything needed for fishing – the boats, sails, nets and gear – was
made in the village and the women did a big share of the work. At the
end of the fishing season the fishermen would supplement their
meagre income by carrying seaweed for sale to farmers or bringing
turf from Connemara to Galway.

The Claddagh was very much a self-sufficient community with
little interest in land. In consequence the village evolved in a haphaz-
ard way according to the changing needs of the population. It possessed no apparent formal layout or structure and comprised a series
of lanes and open green areas with the houses scattered around them
like pieces of a crazy jigsaw. In 1820 it was estimated that there were
up to 3,000 people living there in 400 thatched dwellings. They
formed an independent community with their own way of doing
things. But such independence held within it the seeds of its own
destruction. Despite the best efforts of the Dominican friars and
others to encourage them to adopt new fishing techniques in the
nineteenth century, the villagers steadfastly held onto the traditional

ways. In 1836 the Claddagh had 105 open sailboats and eighty row boats manned by 820 hands. By 1870 there were only 200 'stalwart fishermen' in the village. The demise of the Claddagh is attributable to a number of factors, not least of which was the decline in fish stocks in the bay and the advent of new fishing companies using trawlers, but more especially to the reluctance of the fishermen to adopt new practices. And in the massive havoc that followed on the years of the Great Famine many were forced to sell their boats and emigrate. By the turn of the twentieth century only seventy-three of the 738 inhabitants described themselves as fishermen.

The Irish language had thrived here on the very doorstep of the English-speaking world, but it too failed to survive the breaking up of the community, the decline in the population and the march of prog- ress which eventually joined the Salthill suburbs with the city. The building of a bridge (on the site of the present Wolfe Tone Bridge) in the middle of the nineteenth century gave its inhabitants access to the town and further reduced its physical and cultural separateness. And as the city spread westward it was inevitable that the living con- ditions within this area should come under the watchful eye of the local authorities. In 1927 the medical officer for the western district reported on 'the unsanitary condition of the Claddagh' and declared it an 'unhealthy area' within the meaning of the Housing of the Work- ing Classes Act (1890). Two years later a compulsory purchase order was made by the local Urban District Council in respect of all the houses and in the years following the old dwellings were gradually replaced by new ones. The last thatched house was pulled down in 1938 and the scheme was completed in 1951. And so the physical evi- dence of this fishing village disappeared, and with the death of its last king or mayor, Eoin Concannon, in 1954 (aged ninety), another chapter came to a close. But one custom still survives. Each August the traditional Blessing of the Bay and Boats is carried out by the Dominican fathers – a continuing link between the thriving suburb of today and the unique little fishing village of the past.

THE CLADDAGH RING

Almost everyone in Ireland today is familiar with the name if not the design of the Claddagh ring. It consists of two hands presenting or holding between them a heart, which is surmounted by a crown. Rings with the device of hands clasped together in a sign of friend-ship or utilising a heart as the central motif between two hands have been in use since Roman times and are generally known as *fede* or faith rings. What is remarkable about the design of the Claddagh ring is the fact that a crown sits directly on top of the heart.

The Claddagh ring, this example dates from *c*.1900.

The justification for the name 'Claddagh' ring is attributable to its use as a wedding ring by the people of the Claddagh (*see* above). In particular, the publication in 1843 of Mr & Mrs Hall's *Ireland: its scenery and character* contributed to the association of the name Claddagh with this particular ring design. However, the ring was worn not just by the Claddagh people at that time but by many of the natives of the Connemara and Galway districts. It is noteworthy that the great Galway historian James Hardiman (who gives a detailed account of the Claddagh in his *History of Galway*, published in 1820) makes no mention of the ring as something peculiar to the people who lived there, though he does record a tale about a Galway gold-smith, Richard Joyce, whose name has entered the local folk tradi-tion as the original instigator of the design.

The story relates how shortly after the accession of William III to the throne of England in 1689, the king arranged for the release of British subjects who were then in captivity in Algiers. Among those set free was Richard Joyce, a native of Galway, who had been cap-tured by an Algerian corsair and sold into slavery fourteen years ear-lier. Purchased by a wealthy Turk who followed the profession of a goldsmith, Joyce was instructed in this trade. After his release he returned to Galway where he married and followed this business with considerable success. Whatever about the accuracy of the story there is no doubt that a goldsmith of the name Richard Joyce worked in Galway in the early eighteenth century and there are a number of surviving pieces of plate which bear his stamped initials and trademark: the anchor. Although it is not altogether impossible that it was Joyce who brought together the various motifs and unified them in a single design, nonetheless of the four earliest examples of rings of the Claddagh type, which can be dated to around 1700, only one can be attributed directly to him. The other three are reliably assigned to Thomas Meade, a goldsmith working in Kinsale, County Cork. It was here too that the motif – the two hands clasping a crowned heart – was incorporated in the carving of a wooden chair, which is dated to around 1760. It would appear then that this design had gained a certain currency in the repertoire of some Irish artisans in the eighteenth century. But it became especially popular for use on rings in the Galway region in the later part of that century. This is evident from the surviving examples, which bear the punched initials of George Robinson and Austin French, two goldsmiths who worked in the town in the period around 1784–1800.

The popularity of the ring continued in the west and at the turn of the twentieth century the limits of the district over which it was then worn stretched from the Aran Islands, through Connemara and Joyce country to Galway and its immediate hinterland. It is really only within the last fifty years that the charm of the design has appealed to so many, although this probably owes a considerable debt to the marketing skills of Galway jewellers: creating one especially for Queen Victoria and presenting rings to two American presidents (John F Kennedy, 1963; Ronald Reagan, 1984) has ensured that its fame would reach a wider audience.

It is perhaps worth mentioning some of the so-called traditions associated with the wearing of the ring. One relates that in the Claddagh village they were handed down from mother to daughter, but recent research has pointed out that all surviving Claddagh rings made prior to 1840 are male rings. Some claim that when a ring is worn by a girl on her right hand with the heart pointing towards the nail it means that she is seeking a partner for marriage. Worn on the left hand in a similar position signifies that she is betrothed. On

marriage the ring is turned around and is worn with the heart pointing inwards towards the knuckle. Whatever the truth or fancy in
these traditions they have gained a certain credence in the local folk
tradition and are now part and parcel of the story that is the
Claddagh ring.

EYRE SQUARE

Eyre Square is very much the focal point of the city and has been
since earliest times. It originated as a large open space in front of the
main gate of the medieval town, which was kept free of buildings for
reasons of defence. Like many open spaces in towns and villages it
was known simply as The Green and came to be used as a place for
assembly and games. The town gallows were situated at the top or
northern end (in the area of the present car park), and here too stood
a market cross. Indeed markets and fairs were held at the square's
northern end on a regular basis until the middle of the twentieth century when they were moved to another site (known locally as the Fair
Green, now a car park) near the railway terminus.

A market at Eyre Square, c.1910.

An early attempt at beautifying the central park area is recorded in 1631. The mayor for that year, Sir Valentine Blake, planted it with ash trees and enclosed it with wooden railings. Unfortunately, his efforts did not survive the troubled years of the mid-seventeenth century wars. Throughout the eighteenth century it was still known as The Green, but in 1801 General Meyrick, the military governor of Galway, enclosed it with a stone wall to make a parade ground for soldiers and it then became known as Meyrick Square. This was superseded around 1820 by its present name, Eyre Square, called after the Eyre family who had substantial property holdings on this side of town.

The parade ground established by General Meyrick underwent a major transformation in the early 1840s when it was enclosed with wrought-iron railings and developed as a classic Georgian-type square with a landscaped interior planted with trees. It underwent a further dramatic metamorphosis in the 1960s. In line with modernist thinking the railings were removed and the enclosed area reduced in size to accommodate car parking. The design is now less successful than when first conceived for the central space is no longer the green haven of tranquillity that it was intended to be. This park was reopened in 1965 and named John F Kennedy Memorial Park in honour of the American president who had received the freedom of the city here a few months before his assassination in 1963. A small plaque commemorating this event stands beside the fountain.

Most of the buildings on Eyre Square date to the nineteenth century. Among the more noteworthy is the Bank of Ireland building at the northern end, which was built in the earlier part of the century. Beside it a late Georgian or early Victorian façade now fronts the bulky, concrete Hibernian House; from 1842 until 1973 this building housed the Galway County Club. At the southern end of the Square is another branch of the Bank of Ireland. This neo-classical Italianate building was erected in 1863 and began life as the National Bank.

From earliest times there were inns on this side of the town where travellers could rest overnight while they waited for the gates to open in the morning, and there are still many such establishments here today. The most impressive is the towering Great Southern Hotel, built in 1851–1853 at a cost of £30,000 for the Midland and Great Western Railway Company beside the terminus of their newly constructed railway line. Both were designed by the company's architect, John Skipton Mulvany. The building was first named simply the Railway Hotel. This was changed to its present name following the merger, in 1925, of the various railway companies in the south of Ireland into the Great Southern Railway Company. At the opposite end is the Imperial Hotel, originally established in 1810 as The Clanricarde Arms. Built into its façade is a plaque bearing the coat of arms of Galway, which probably came from one of the large bastioned out-works constructed in the mid-seventeenth century to protect the town on this side. One of the most recent additions is the Eyre Square Centre, a two-storey shopping complex-cum-apartments opened in 1991, which incorporates part of the old town wall.

Being an open space, it was natural that the square should become the site for various public memorials. The two large cannon (sixty-four pounders), which now point menacingly at the Bank of Ireland on the esplanade at its northern end, were brought to Galway in 1857 having been captured during the Crimean War (1854–1856) at the Battle of Inkerman. In 1873 a bronze statue of a County Galway landlord, Lord Dunkellin (d.1867), was erected here. It was pulled down by some angry citizens in June 1922, dragged through the streets of the town and thrown into the docks: they were protesting against the lack of housing and tenants' rights. Its position was subsequently taken by a memorial more befitting the emerging State – the almost life-size statue of one of Ireland's most famous writers in the Irish language, Pádraic Ó Conaire (1882–1928), by Albert Power, RHA, unveiled in 1935. Ó Conaire was a native of Galway and wrote numerous short stories and books, including *Deóraíocht* (*Exile*, telling of his years in London) and *M'asal beag dubh* (*My little black donkey,* an animal that accompanied him on his many travels around Ireland). The inscription on the plaque at his foot reads in translation: 'Pádraic Ó Conaire, true Irishman and renowned author in the Irish language.'

The Browne Doorway, which now stands rather forlornly at the top of the Square, was moved here in 1905–1906 from a house in Abbeygate Street Lower. Preserved as an example of the architectural heritage of the city it was inserted as the principal entrance to the square. Directly above the door is a panel, dated 1627, with the coats of arms of husband and wife Martin Browne and Marie Lynch, flanked by stylised carvings of dragon-like creatures. The doorway is very typical of the classical style of Jacobean architecture that became fashionable in Galway in the early seventeenth century. Nearby is the statue of Liam Mellowes (unveiled in 1957), who led a short but effective rising in the county in 1916 and who represented Galway in the first and second Dáil Éireann (Irish Parliament) in 1919–1922. He was executed during the Irish Civil War on 8 December 1922.

Statue of Liam Mellowes by Domhnall Ó Muchadha (1957).

Without doubt, the most impressive monument in the square is the Quincentenial Fountain, erected in 1984 to celebrate the 500th anniversary of the formal establishment of Galway corporation. It was designed by Eamon O'Doherty and consists of a series of sheets of Corten steel mounted so as to recall the sails of the Galway Hooker. The natural rust evokes the dark brown colour of the sail cloth used on these vessels.

Eyre Square is scheduled for further change and modernisation. New proposals are now before the citizens, which are set to transform this space for the new millennium.

'SPANISH ARCH' AND FISH MARKET

The name 'Spanish Arch' is a completely modern invention. This section of the town wall was formerly known by its Irish name, *An Poirse Caoch* (the Blind Arch), because one of the two surviving arches was closed. Indeed, this earlier name only dates from the late seventeenth century and appears to have come into use after 1688 when the corporation converted a jetty, which extended southwards along the line of present-day Long Walk, into a pier. In so doing, they broke through one of the arches to gain access to this extension. The 'Spanish' element of the present name was borrowed from a former small square to the east. That square became known in the eighteenth century as the Spanish Parade – a romantic throw-back to the times when Galway had extensive trading contacts with Spain. This area at the quay originally was called simply The Parade. It ceased to exist as a square proper in 1993 when the houses along its southern side were demolished to make way for a new access road.

A drawing by Thomas Phillips of the quay area in 1685.

The old name for the Spanish Arch is *Ceann an bhaile* or the head of the wall (i.e., of the walled town). Originally there were four arches here, though only the two outermost survive. It is not known precisely when they were built, but this section of the town wall was converted into some form of fortification about 1586–1588. The arches originally fronted onto the old quays of the town and the present paved area now occupies their site; the rather large Port More development runs along the line of the old town wall. There is a very fine stretch of the old town wall at the rear of the arches, which may be compared with the remarkable pen-picture of this area drawn by Thomas Phillips in 1685. The quays were the hub of the town's commerce in the medieval and early modern periods and remained in use until the present docks were opened in 1840; the quays were filled in shortly after.

The arches and adjoining buildings were acquired by Galway corporation in 1972, with the cooperation of Bord Fáilte, and part of the premises was converted for use as a museum. This house was formerly the home of sculptress Clare Sheridan who lived here in the 1940s and early 1950s. It was she who obtained the fine portals which adorn the entrance to the museum from an old mansion at Ardfry, across the bay. A first cousin of both Sir Winston Churchill and the celebrated County Monaghan author Sir Shane Leslie, she led a colourful and exciting life. Her extensive travels included romantic dalliances with such notables as Leon Trotsky, Benito Mussolini and Charlie Chaplin! She was a noted sculptress, though there are only two of her carvings in Galway: the so-called Madonna of the Quays, who looks down from the window above the entrance to the museum, and the wooden crucifix in the Church of Christ the King at Salthill. Moves are afoot to establish the museum in more suitable premises and this is badly needed for the present building is cramped and overcrowded. Among the many items illustrating the history of the city are some fine pieces of carved stonework. The visitor should also go out onto the roof-top terrace above the arches from where there are wonderful views along the river and estuary.

The large open area in front of the museum is known as the Fish Market. This name dates from the early nineteenth century when a small building was erected at its northern end (just in front of present-day Jury's Inn) for regulating the sale of fresh fish. After the infilling of the old quays and the erection of a wooden bridge (on the site of Wolfe Tone Bridge) in the mid-nineteenth century, this whole area developed into a bustling open market. It was here that the Claddagh women came with their baskets of fish to sell to the citizens of Galway. But all is now changed. The market is long gone and a busy thoroughfare runs through here. The only constant is the cries of seagulls who swoop down to pick up titbits thrown by tourists.

Wolfe Tone Bridge (named after one of the founders of the United Irishmen who had close connections with Galway) was built in 1934 and is the third bridge on this site. The first, a wooden structure, was erected as an interim measure in 1850 while the present O'Brien Bridge was being built. The temporary bridge was found to be most useful and, accordingly, was left in place; it was replaced by an iron one in 1887. To the north of the bridge stands an old fisheries watchtower, built in 1853 and now converted into a small fisheries museum. Beside the bridge is a modern piece of sculpture presented to the city in 1992 by the citizens of Genoa, Italy, in commemoration of a visit here by their most famous sailor and explorer, Christopher Columbus. The inscription on the plinth reads in translation: 'On this shore around 1477, Christopher Columbus from Genoa had a presentiment of a land far away across the western sea.' Not far away, on the pavement, is a large, roughly hewn block of limestone with a smooth, polished top. The inscribed plaque tells us that it was 'Erected by the Seattle–Galway Sister City Association October 1993' as a symbol of the ties between the respective cities. It is 'marked with the geophysical data of the City of Seattle' and there is 'another stone in Seattle marked with the geophysical data of the City of Galway'! And finally, it is worth mentioning two other items that might escape the attention of the casual visitor. In the lounge bar attached to Jury's Inn are two of the finest decorated fireplace lintels from the city (dated 1575 and 1645).

THE COUNTY COURTHOUSE AND TOWN HALL THEATRE

The Town Hall Theatre began life as the town courthouse and was sited at Newtownsmith for the very same reason as the county court-house directly opposite it. They were built here to be near their respective jails, which were situated on Nuns' Island, on the other side of the river (on the site of the present cathedral and car park). Both the town and county jails were located in the town in the open-ing years of the nineteenth century. Part of the sixteenth-century Tholsel in Mainguard Street was used as the town jail, and Blake's Castle in Quay Street served as the county jail. Following the passing of an Act of Parliament (1802) work commenced on the construction of a new county jail in 1804. Three years later the grand jury for the

The county courthouse, Salmon Weir Bridge and the jail (1820).

town successfully petitioned to have the act amended and, in consequence, a new town jail was built adjoining that for the county. The
entire complex was enclosed within a massive stone wall some six
metres (twenty feet) high. The prisoners in the old Tholsel jail were
moved into their new building in 1810 and those in Blake's Castle
were transferred to the new county jail towards the middle of the following year. Both jails were amalgamated into one after 1877, when
the control of prisons was taken away from their respective grand
juries and vested in a new General Prisons Board.

Work began on building the county courthouse in 1812 and it was
opened three years later. The architect was Richard Morrison who is
noted for his many country houses as well as other courthouses and
jails. He had already supervised the building of the county jail and his
design for the courthouse is very much typical of the classical style
then in vogue for public buildings. The entrance is beneath a
Grecian-style portico with a massive entablature. Above each of the
Doric pillars he placed his favourite ornamental motif: the lion mask.

Detail of 1816 carving.

The portico was topped by a carving of the royal coat of arms of the
house of Hanover, which were taken down after Independence, being
considered inappropriate to an emerging State, and re-erected in the
grounds of the university where they may still be seen.

The building was not long open when it became the subject for a
most unusual form of graffiti. Two crosses, dated 1816, were carved
on the panels on either side of the main door. The right-hand cross

sits on the horizontal bar of the monogram IHS and is accompanied by the name I Healy. The left-hand cross sits on a pyramidal base and is unsigned. These are two of many similar crosses that were carved around this time on various walls and buildings in the city; there are two more on the Aran Islands and one at Menlough village, just north of Galway. Many of these carvings are dated, ranging from 1815–1818 (1816 being the commonest), and a number have the name I Healy carved alongside. In one instance the carver gives his first name as John and we may take it that the 'I' on the courthouse example is the initial of the Latin form of his name: Iohannes. Who John Healy was or why he chose to be remembered in this way is a complete mystery as, indeed, is how he managed to carve these without being detected for they were all done with hammer and chisel: he must have been an exceptionally quiet worker! He even succeeded in leaving his tell-tale 'signature' on the west end of St Nicholas's Church, where two other examples can be seen. It has been suggested that they commemorate the laying of the foundation stone in 1816 of the former Pro-Cathedral in Middle Street, but other than the fact that many share a similar date there is no evidence to support this and their origin and purpose still remain unknown.

From the outset it had been intended that the county jail and courthouse should be connected by a bridge (the present Salmon Weir Bridge) and one of the conditions of the 1807 amended act specified that the grand jury for the town was to contribute to the cost of erecting it. Although its construction did not get under way until 1818, it was completed within a year.

For many years the town grand jury had been considering building their own courthouse, but for various reasons this had never been carried into effect. Now that a bridge was in place linking Newtown-smith with Nuns' Island (where the new town jail stood), the former area was the obvious choice for the building. Appropriately, a site fronting the county courthouse was selected and the foundations laid in June 1824. A local Galway architect, Alexander Hay, was responsible for its design, which imitates (though on a less grand scale) that of the county courthouse opposite. Although completed by the summer of the following year, the grand jury prudently decided to postpone holding the summer assizes there in August, considering it sensible to wait until the structure had safely dried out. The building served the dual function of both courthouse and town hall and was the venue for many public assemblies and social gatherings in the nineteenth century. By 1885 it had ceased to function as a court-house proper – all the courts then being held in the county court-house – and so the town commissioners decided to use it solely as a town hall or theatre. For much of the twentieth century it housed a cinema.

Both courthouse buildings were completely refurbished in the mid-1990s and the central area of Courthouse Square was land-scaped as part of Galway corporation's environmental improvement plans. The newly restored Town Hall Theatre was officially opened on 1 February 1996, and the first performance – the premier of Martin McDonagh's 'The Beauty Queen of Leenane' – was given by the city's renowned troupe, the Druid Theatre Company.

IHS TILES

The visitor to Galway will notice that over the doorways of many houses are small, square, blue-and-yellow tiles. If you look closely you will notice that they bear the monogram IHS surrounded by a circle of flaming rays. The origin of these tiles can be traced back to a retreat given by a Franciscan priest, Fr Francis Donnelly, to the Poor Clare nuns of Galway in 1913, when he preached on the power of the Holy Name as advocated by St Bernadine of Sienna (*d*.1444). St Ber-nadine had made much use of the name Jesus as a symbol of the Lord himself, using as a badge the monogram IHS (from the Greek form of the name). It occurred to Fr Donnelly that something could be done under the patronage of the Holy Name to stem the then prevalent problem of drunkenness, and in the following year he estab-lished a temperance society in Cork. The organisation grew rapidly and, encouraged by its success, Fr Donnelly turned his attention to the idea of putting the monogram

An IHS tile.

of the Holy Name over the doors of houses, as preached by St Bernadine. Although the First World War was then in progress he managed to procure a large quantity of tiles and the devotion quickly spread throughout all the cities and towns where the Franciscan order had houses. Fr Donnelly continued to preach and promote devotion to the Holy Name until his death in 1929.

AN TAIBHDHEARC

Close to the Augustinian church in Middle Street is the small theatre known as An Taibhdhearc, the only one in Ireland that is devoted entirely to the production of plays in the Irish language. You will not find the word *taibhdhearc* in any modern Irish-English dictionary, but it is a genuine Irish word nonetheless and was carefully chosen by the original founders. It occurs in an early ninth-century Irish manuscript, the Book of Armagh, as a marginal gloss on the New Testament. The Latin word *theatrum* is there translated as *taibderc* (modernised as *taibhdhearc*), which is a combination of two words: *taibhse*, meaning spectacle/ghost, and *dearc*, meaning behold!

The roots of An Taibhdhearc go back to the early twentieth century when an enthusiastic group of local dramatists managed to persuade the then Minister for Finance Ernest Blythe (the man who is more usually remembered for his parsimony in reducing the old age pension from ten shillings (fifty pence) to nine shillings (forty-five pence)) to finance their proposed Irish theatre. In 1928 the local committee leased what was then known as the Augustinian Hall and the company has been in residence here ever since. During the summer of that year two of Ireland's emerging *dramatis personae*, Micheál Mac Liammóir (*d.*1978), then aged twenty-nine, and Hilton Edwards (*d.*1982), aged twenty-five, best remembered for founding Dublin's Gate Theatre, were asked to equip the new Taibhdhearc and produce its first play. Hilton did the lighting system and Micheál painted the walls and sets, including the beautiful black curtains with their golden interlaced designs, a replica of which still hangs on the stage. The first play was Mac Liammóir's own 'Diarmuid agus Gráinne', which opened on 27 August 1928. Over the following three years Mac Liammóir and Edwards continued to produce plays there on an intermittent basis.

An Taibhdhearc.

Since that time An Taibhdhearc has witnessed the production of many original works and translations of the great plays of the world, both classical and contemporary. Only in exceptional cases has a production in the English language ever been staged there, the most notable being Mac Liammóir's own tribute to Oscar Wilde, 'The Importance of Being Oscar'. Other notable personages who have been connected with this theatre include one of Galway's best-known writers, Walter Macken (d.1967), as actor and producer, and the internationally renowned actress, Siobhán McKenna (d.1986) who made her début here in 1940 while studying at Galway university.

THE NORA BARNACLE HOUSE MUSEUM

The house at number 8 Bowling Green has been turned into a little museum in honour of Nora Barnacle, companion and wife of the poet, novelist and playwright James Joyce (1882–1941). Born in Galway in March 1884, Nora grew up and worked in the city before moving to Dublin in 1904. On 16 June of that year she went out for the first time with the young aspiring writer, a date he later immortalised as Bloomsday in his most famous work, *Ulysses*. Nora and Joyce left Ireland the following September and lived the rest of their

The Nora Barnacle House Museum.

lives on the continent, returning only for brief visits. In 1909 Joyce visited Nora's mother at the house in Bowling Green. Three years later Nora and Joyce visited together, and during their stay went to the old cemetery at Rahoon on the outskirts of Galway, where one of Nora's early boyfriends, Michael 'Sonny' Bodkin, lies buried. Her account of his untimely death from tuberculosis in 1900 had prompted Joyce to incorporate it as a motif in his story 'The Dead', and a plaque now marks the house in Prospect Hill where the Bodkins had a sweetshop. Nora did not return to Bowling Green again until April 1922, which was to be her last visit to Galway. Nora survived her husband by ten years and died in Zürich on 10 April 1951.

THE CATHEDRAL

When the diocese of Galway was established in 1831 the local parish chapel of St Nicholas in Middle Street (built 1816–1821) was designated the Pro-Cathedral. This, however, was considered too small and in 1876 a fund was established for the erection of a more suitable church. Shortly before 1909 the site of the old Shambles Barracks at O'Brien Bridge (where the Patrician boys' primary school stands) was purchased and plans drawn up for the work. However, other diocesan needs were found to be more pressing and nothing further happened until 1937 when Michael Browne was appointed bishop. It was he who had the determination and purpose to realise the aspirations of his predecessors.

The original barrack site was deemed unsuitable as it was too small and (with a certain foresight) lacked adequate car parking

spaces. In 1941 the site of the old county and town jails on Nuns'
Island (closed two years previously by the government) was transferred to Galway county council and they in turn handed it over for a
nominal sum to Bishop Browne for the proposed cathedral. By the
end of the year the old jails had been demolished but no further work
was undertaken until after the Second World War. The design for the
project was given to John J Robinson of Dublin and the foundation
stone was blessed on 25 October 1957. Work commenced on the
building in the following February and the whole structure was completed seven years later. The total cost, including furnishing, was
almost one million pounds. Regrettably, Robinson did not live to see
his building finished for he died in January 1965. The cathedral was
dedicated later that year on the Feast of the Assumption (15 August)
by Cardinal Richard Cushing of Boston, who had been appointed official Papal Legate for the occasion. It was named The Cathedral of
Our Lady Assumed into Heaven and St Nicholas, after the patrons of
the Galway diocese and the old Catholic parish in the city.

Galway cathedral from the air, shortly after its opening in 1965.

The cathedral is, without doubt, the most outstanding public monument constructed in Galway in the twentieth century and is a significant landmark on its skyline. Standing on a long, narrow island that is bounded by the River Corrib on one side and the smaller Gaol River (now gradually changing to the Cathedral River) on the other, the building was erected on an approximate north–south axis, with the entrance at the north. It was positioned so that the dome would be situated on the centre-line of the Salmon Weir Bridge as one approaches from the city. Recalling Galway's historic trading links with Spain, the architect sought inspiration in the classical Renaissance tradition of the Iberian peninsula. In consequence, the building is almost totally foreign in style and owes little or nothing to the native Irish Romanesque or Gothic traditions. Although its architecture defies classification, the structure is both dignified and spacious and glories in magnificent works by the finest Irish ecclesiastical artists of the later twentieth century, including Imogen Stuart (bronzework, main entrance), Patrick Pollen (mosaics and stained-glass), Gabrielle O'Riordan

At the opening of Galway Cathedral, 15 August 1965: Bishop Michael Browne, Cardinal Richard Cushing, Boston, and Mr Brendan Holland, mayor of Galway.

(stations of the cross), Aengus Buckley (frescos), Domhnaill Ó Murchada (sacrament carvings, main entrance) and Phyllis Burke, George Campbell, Gillian Deeney, Roisín Dowd Murphy, Patrick Heney, John Murphy, James Scanlon, George Walshe and Manus Walshe (stained-glass).

The cathedral has a traditional cruciform design with a central dome above the crossing, beneath which is the high altar. Its northern end is flanked by two bell-towers surmounted by copulas and the baptistery is positioned on the ground floor of the western tower.

There is seating for about 1,500 persons and up to 1,000 more can be accommodated standing in the aisles. The walls are of limestone, which was quarried from sites near Galway and Ballinasloe, and the roof and dome are covered in copper. The barrel-vaulted coffered ceiling is of American cedarwood, and the flooring of the central passage and aisles is of sepia Connemara marble with red, white and green insets. The pews are made from West African mahogany and the floor below them is of red tile with the central heating running directly underneath. It was originally intended that the high altar would have a baldachino or canopy over it, but this was never carried into effect.

Most visitors enter by the doorway in the east transept, facing the Salmon Weir Bridge. Above this entrance is a large plate-glass panel with an engraving of the **Last Judgement**. The three bronze doors comprising the main northern entrance include scenes from the gospels and events from the early life of the Church. The tympana or recesses above contain carvings depicting the sacraments of Baptism, Matrimony and Holy Orders. Among the chief features of the spacious interior are the wonderful mosaics, the great **Crucifixion** on the south gable, the inscription *Gloria in excelcis Deo et in terra pax hominibus bonae voluntatis* (Glory to God in the highest and in earth, peace, good will towards men) along the dome collar with the archangels in supporting triangular pendentives, **St Joseph the Worker** in the shrine in the nave and the **Resurrection** in the mortuary chapel. The Resurrection is flanked by portrait roundels of the Irish patriot Patrick Pearse (on Christ's right) who had close links with the west of Ireland, and the less-than-saintly president of the United States John F Kennedy (on Christ's left!), who had been made a freeman of the city only a few months before his death in 1963.

The rose windows – and they are genuinely rose-shaped – dominate three of the four gables. Each presents the mysteries of the rosary: Joyful (nave), Sorrowful (east transept) and Glorious (west transept). The remaining stained-glass windows are devoted to biblical figures and events and were finally completed in 1999. Those on the upper level present the Old Testament, while those at ground level depict scenes from the life of Christ. The great organ, by Rushworth and Dreaper, Liverpool, contains over 3,000 pipes and has forty-five speaking stops (independent tones). An international organ festival is held each year in the cathedral during July and August.

The cathedral has four opposing side chapels: the **Chapel of St Nicholas** (originally intended as a Lady chapel, now serving as the Blessed Sacrament chapel), the **Mortuary chapel** and the **chapels of St Colman and St Fachnan**, the patron saints of the neighbouring dioceses of Kilmacduagh and Kilfenora, respectively (since 1883 both have been under the jurisdiction of the Bishop of Galway). Each of the last two chapels mentioned contains a fresco representing a scene from the lives of the saints. Of particular interest is the reredos above the altar in the Chapel of St Nicholas, which consists of four limestone panels arranged to represent the Coronation of Our Lady by the Holy Trinity. Three of these date to the mid-seventeenth century (God the Father, God the Son, Blessed Virgin) while the fourth (Holy Ghost) is modern. The older panels came from the Pro-Cathedral in Middle Street, where they had been transferred from St Nicholas's Church. Originally they probably were intended to form part of an altar- or tomb-surround that was never completed. The panel depicting God the Father formerly contained, to the right of the figure, the unfinished carvings of a dove and an angel with a censor. Regrettably, these were removed when the panels were re-erected here. On the west wall of this chapel is a bronze bust of Bishop Michael Browne. After an exceptionally long episcopate (1937–1976), Bishop Browne died in 1980 and his remains, together with those of his three predecessors, lie in the crypt beneath the Chapel of St Nicholas.

No tour of the cathedral would be complete without a brief visit to the southern end of the adjoining car park where a small, raised area with an inset paved cross marks the spot where the remains of the inmates of the former jails were interred.

THE UNIVERSITY

Since the passing of the Universities Act in 1997, the university colleges of Galway, Cork, Dublin and Maynooth now constitute the National University of Ireland (NUI), and the older, abbreviated title UCG is giving way to its newer counterpart, NUI Galway. At present there are in excess of 11,000 students attending the university, which is spread out over a campus that must be one of the most attractively located in Ireland, encompassing some 105 hectares (260 acres) along the banks of the River Corrib.

It has come a long way since it first opened its doors in 1849 to the sixty-eight students enroled in its faculties of Arts, Law, Medicine and Engineering. The college has had a somewhat chequered history, successfully surviving three attempts at closure: in the mid-1870s, in the early 1900s and in 1926. It owes its existence to Sir Robert Peel (better known as the originator of The Peelers, Ireland's first police force, in 1822), who, as prime minister, oversaw the introduction of the Academical Institutions (Ireland) Bill in Parliament in 1845. The university was formally brought into existence at the end of that year and instituted under the title Queen's College, Galway.

Galway university, aerial photo taken c.1955.

The design for the project was by the distinguished architect Joseph B Keane, Dublin, noted for numerous churches, courthouses and country houses. As befitted an institute of learning, Keane chose a Tudor-style period design (considered to have been inspired by Christ Church College, Oxford), which consists of a symmetrical scheme built around a central quadrangle. In line with earlier practices, a substantial portion of the building was taken up with residences for the president and vice-president. The ceremony of the turning of the first sod was carried out in 1846, and though unfinished the college was officially opened on 30 October 1849. Built during the years of the Great Famine the building work brought much-needed employment to the tradesmen of the town.

From the outset Peel intended that the new colleges be 'undenominational'. In this he drew the wrath of Cardinal Newman and the Catholic hierarchy who condemned them as 'Godless Colleges'. But Peel had his way and, despite the directive prohibiting Catholics from entering these institutions, there was a healthy mix of different denominations among the student body in its early years. Indeed, it is noteworthy that its first president, Dr Joseph William Kirwan, was an eminent Roman Catholic divine and parish priest of Kilcummin (Oughterard). From its foundation the college was very much a male preserve. Females were not admitted until 1888 and then only to the faculty of Arts! It was to be some years before the other faculties allowed them access.

Queen's College, Galway, underwent two further name changes. In 1882 it was reconstituted as part of the Royal University of Ireland, and this was replaced in 1908 by a new act establishing two separate universities, one to be called the Queen's University of Belfast and the other (comprising the colleges of Cork, Dublin and Galway) to be known as the National University of Ireland. In 1929 an act was passed by the new Irish government specifically relating to the Galway college, which stipulated that 'an increasing proportion of the academic and administrative functions ... be performed through the medium of Irish', an obligation the college has sought consistently to fulfil. The act also resulted in a significant change to the composition of the student body for the Galway university now became a genuine all-Ireland institution as students, attracted by the scholarships on offer, came here from all over the country.

Since its foundation the university has been an intrinsic part of the social fabric of Galway and the city's growth is directly linked to its development. The students have always brought vibrancy, both economic and cultural, to the city and many of Galway's great cultural successes – Druid Theatre, Macnas, the Galway Arts Festival and Cúirt – can trace their roots to the university. The fact that Galway is now the Irish-language media capital of Ireland is attributable in no small way to the presence of the university, where the language is a distinguishing feature of its identity.

It was not until the 1960s that the college began to expand beyond the confines of the Quad (Quadrangle) as the old building is affectionately known. A new range of Arts buildings was begun in the 1970s on the banks of the Corrib and the design, by architects Scott Tallon Walker, is very much within the Modernist tradition of utilitarian architecture. It is built up by the repetition of a single modular unit and the cubic blend of steel, glass and concrete reflect, in their materials and colours, the sombre beiges and browns of the Connemara landscape. The main entrance is elevated on a terrace-like podium approached by a flight of steps: here sits the brightly painted sheet-metal sculpture that is symbolic of the Celtic knot. This new range includes the James Hardiman Library (1782–1855, and librarian here from 1848), which counts among its manuscript collections the early municipal records of Galway corporation (1485–1818). Additional blocks were added in the 1980s and 1990s as the college continued to expand and develop. Other recent additions to the campus include Árus na Gaeilge, a dedicated Irish-language facility,

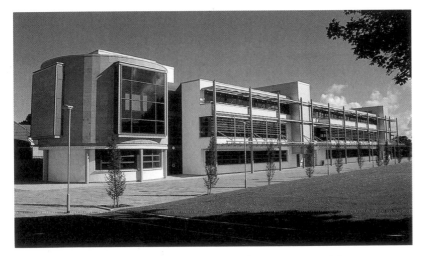

Modern materials for modern times: the new Regional Centre for Modern Languages at NUI Galway.

the Martin Ryan Marine Science Institute (Ireland's leading centre in marine science and technology), opened 1992, and the Regional Centre for Modern Languages (completed 1999) beside the newly refurbished entrance on Newcastle Road. The whole face of the university is gradually changing as academics and researchers now work in partnership with other institutions, industries and commercial enterprises in the region, thus ensuring the continued growth and prosperity of both town and gown.

FORTHILL

A cemetery now marks the site of a huge star-shaped or bastioned fort that stood on the headland above the entrance to Lough Atalia (Loch an tSáile – the saltwater lake) some 250 metres south of the old walled town. Only the name, Forthill, serves to remind us of its former existence. Begun in 1602 – the year following the disastrous defeat of the Irish and Spanish forces at the Battle of Kinsale – the fort was built by order of Queen Elizabeth I as much to protect the town and its harbour as to overawe its citizens, some of whose sympathies were seen to lie outside the realm. The fort incorporated the

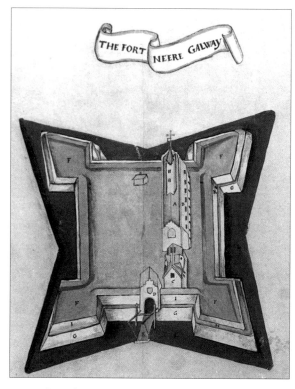

Plan of St Augustine's Fort by Josias Bodley, drawn some time between 1608 and 1611.

site of the old Augustinian friary, founded in 1508, and because of this association became known as St Augustine's Fort.

The fort was typical of the period and reflected contemporary European ideas in design and construction. It was a substantial work (measuring some sixty metres square with walls over seven metres high) with diamond-shaped bastions at the corners and surrounded by a wide, deep fosse. The Augustinian church was retained for use as a garrison chapel and storehouse, while the commander and his officers were housed in a separate building. The ordinary soldiers had to content themselves with lean-to structures built against the walls of the church. When completed, the fort must have presented a most imposing sight and throughout its forty-year existence it dominated the town and harbour.

Shortly after the outbreak of the 1641 rebellion, St Augustine's Fort became the centre of a bitter row between the largely Catholic and pro-Royalist townspeople and the Protestant and pro-Parliamentarian commander of the garrison. Eventually the fort was taken by the townspeople in 1643 and demolished. The old church, however, was spared and restored to the Augustinian friars, but its commanding position remained a major concern for the military leaders in the town who feared that it might be used by a besieging army. Accordingly, it was pulled down two years later.

Given its earlier ecclesiastical associations, the site was regarded by the local Catholic population as sacred ground and they gradually began to use it as a place of burial in the eighteenth century. Almost mid-way along the east boundary wall of the present cemetery is a graveslab recording this event: 'We earnestly begg dear Christians to say one Ave Maria for the soul of John Bodkin of Anagh, his wife Megg Blake of Ardfry and their posterity. This was the first tomb made in this abbey in the year 1745.' Notwithstanding this testament, we know that the Augustinian friars were buried here from as early as 1727, and it seems likely that the Bodkin–Blake memorial was a formal recognition of an established practice. As the burials increased on the hill the local landlord became concerned and had the upper section enclosed as a cemetery proper in 1811; this was later extended southwards to the roadway in 1852.

Set in the east boundary wall, just above the 1745 graveslab noted above, is a plaque commemorating some 300 Spaniards, survivors of the ill-fated Armada, who were taken here in 1588 and summarily executed. According to the seventeenth-century historian and native of Galway Dr John Lynch (d. 1673), the Augustinian friars ministered to the sailors before their deaths. He also records the tradition that two of the survivors were secretly sheltered in the town before returning safely to Spain.

It had long been thought that no physical trace of the great St Augustine's Fort had survived. However, in the course of carrying out some conservation works at the cemetery in 1999, a small portion of the retaining wall of one of the bastions was exposed immediately behind the old mortuary chapel inside the entrance (subsequently covered over). These works have seen the whole cemetery cleaned up, pathways repaired and the mortuary chapel refurbished.

ST AUGUSTINE'S WELL

St Augustine's Well is situated on the foreshore of Lough Atalia and is the last surviving holy well in Galway. At one time there were at least seven such wells in the general vicinity of the town, including one inside the walls (outside the present Custom House, Flood Street) dedicated to St Brendan, patron saint of Annaghdown diocese, in which Galway was situated. The well undoubtedly takes its name from the Augustinian friary, which stood on the site of the nearby Forthill cemetery. There formerly were two other wells near it, dedicated to the Blessed Virgin and to St John the Baptist, but these went out of use in the second half of the nineteenth century. Being tidal, the well is completely submerged at high tide and the only indication of its presence is the top of a cross peeping above the waterline.

This well was the scene for an 'extraordinary cure' that took place on 11 June 1673. A fourteen-year-old boy, Patrick Lynch, who suffered from some form of wasting illness, was brought here as a last resort by his family who had given up all hope of his recovery; his father had even prepared a coffin for him. After being immersed in the well the boy was cured and his family and friends were so convinced that a miracle had taken place that they made a sworn deposition in the presence of the leading Catholic clergy and laity of the

Devotions at St Augustine's Holy Well, as seen through the eyes of the *Illustrated London News*. Note that the perspective is reversed.

town. The well's waters are still regarded as having healing proper-
ties, especially for anyone suffering from eye complaints, and the well
is resorted to on the last Sunday in July (known as Garland Sunday –
the Christianised harvest celebration of the old Celtic festival of
Lughnasa) and on St Augustine's feast-day (28 August). In 1999 the
well was refurbished by the Galway Civic Trust who installed a stone
bench and a new cross.

BOLLINGBROOK FORT

Situated a little over one kilometre northeast of the old walled town
(just off the present Seán Mulvoy Road) are the last remnants of a
series of substantial fortifications erected by the Cromwellian army
during the siege of Galway in the summer of 1651. In order to prevent any relief from getting through to the town from the east, the
Cromwellians constructed a line of earthen fortifications stretching
from bogs along the Terryland River on the north across the main
thoroughfare, Bohermore, to Lough Atalia on the south. These works
included three star-shaped forts of which Bollingbrook Fort was
northernmost. Their principal and largest fort stood beside the
Bohermore Road (on the site of the present New Cemetery) and
there was a similar-sized fort to Bollingbrook Fort erected beyond
this, near present College Road. All three were linked by a series of
earthen banks that included small fortified positions. The Cromwellian army took up their positions in the three forts and eventually,
after a siege lasting nine months, the beleaguered citizens surrendered to them in April 1652. Having served their purpose, the siegeworks were abandoned and the besieging army moved in and took
control of the town.

The forts were to see action again some forty years later during the
war between James II and William of Orange. Although repaired in
1690, the townspeople decided not to use them as part of their
defences against William's army, probably because they were considered to be too distant from the town. Instead they concentrated their
efforts on building large earthen ramparts in front of the existing
town walls. The forts may have been used as base-camps by the
attacking Williamite army who arrived before Galway on 19 July
1691. However, their occupancy was very brief for the town

surrendered two days later. Over the following centuries the earth-works fell to decay and gradually were removed. Only the eastern por-tion of Bollingbrook Fort now survives to tell of the small part played by Galway in the struggle for power between parliament and king.

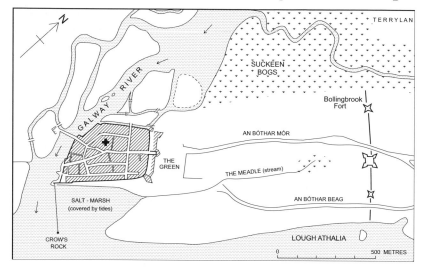

Map showing the location of the siegeworks erected
by the Cromwellian army in 1651.

In plan, Bollingbrook Fort resembled a four-pointed star with curved sides, typical of many such small earthen forts of the period. It measured approximately twenty-eight metres square and was sur-rounded by a wide fosse, over two metres deep. Archaeological exca-vations undertaken on the site have recovered a spur, cannonball and numerous musket balls; we may conjecture that some of these were probably fired or lost during the various engagements that took place during the siege of 1651–1652. The name Bollingbrook Fort post-dates the Cromwellian period and derives from the fact that the land on which it is sited came into the possession of one John Bollingbrook in the later seventeenth century, the area then becom-ing known as Bollingbrook's Parks. The surviving section of the fort was conserved and restored by the Galway Civic Trust in 1999.

TERRYLAND 'CASTLE'

Most people who travel westwards over the River Corrib via the Quin-centenary Bridge probably do not realise that they are crossing the river almost exactly where countless others did in medieval and earlier times. Just south of the bridge there was a ford and anyone travelling on foot or on horseback who wished to avoid having to go through the town had to use this route. Northwards, the river and lake, stretching for over fifty kilometres, presented a very definite barrier. History tells us that the ford was used on many occasions by both the Gaelic Irish and English alike who made incursions into each other's territories for booty.

Two castles stood on either side of the river at this point. On the west was the Newcastle – demolished in the late eighteenth century – while on the east stood Terryland Castle. The present building, strictly speaking, is not a castle as such but rather a fortified house dating from around 1600. The lands in this area were long in the possession of the Clanricard family – descendants of the original Anglo-Norman settlers, the de Burgos – and this house was built for the fourth earl of Clanricard, Richard Burke (1572–1635). It was looked after by one of his agents, Sir Richard Blake (*d.*1663), a prominent Galway landowner. During the troubled years of the 1640s and early 1650s the house was used by the fifth earl, Ulick Burke (1604–1657), as a venue for important meetings and gatherings. The lord deputy, the duke of Ormond, stayed here prior to taking ship for France, and both the papal nuncio, Giovanni Battista Rinuccini (who had come to Ireland to defend the government of the Church on behalf of the pope) and the representative of the duke of Lorraine (whose promise of military aid was not worth the paper it was written on) were received at Terryland. When the Cromwellian army approached Galway, a detachment of soldiers was placed there to defend the house, but fearing the worst they abandoned it and fled downriver to Galway.

Following Galway's surrender in 1652 the earl of Clanricard lost most of his Irish estates, including Terryland, and the house was leased to the Cromwellian Robert Clarke (later Recorder of Galway). In 1655, however, Sir Richard Blake successfully petitioned to have the lease granted to him and he looked after the house until the Clanricards were restored to their former possessions by King Charles II. In 1691 it served as the residence of the second son of the seventh earl, John Burke (created Lord Bophin in 1689). When the Williamites came before Galway in July of that year this was the first house to be attacked. It had been garrisoned by a detachment of French and Irish troops, but on seeing the enemy approach they immediately set it on fire and withdrew by

Terryland 'Castle'.

boat to the town. The building was completely gutted and has been a ruin ever since.

After the war the Clanricards built a new house on the river's edge nearby and this was occupied until the early nineteenth century; a tiny fragment still survives on the other side of the bridge. The remains of their former dwelling, Terryland Castle, which gradually became known as Oldcastle, fell victim to the vandal and wall-builder. In consequence, only a shell survives. Nonetheless, it preserves some interesting features: the typical Jacobean, diamond-shaped chimney stack and gabled dormer windows, and the large kitchen fireplaces with adjoining brick-lined oven. Defensive considerations were not forgotten, as evidenced by the projecting corbels for corner machicolations – defensive, turret-like features at roof level enabling missiles to be hurled on anyone attempting to undermine the foundations below. Originally the house would have been surrounded by a bawn or enclosing wall and history also tells us that it had extensive orchards and gardens. Terryland house was a small but comfortable residence, all in all a fitting retreat for a great earl.